OPERATION AVIARY

Airborne Special Operations - Korea, 1950 - 1953

Colonel Douglas C. Dillard, USA Ret.

www.trafford.com
North America & international
toll-free: 1 888 232 4444 (USA & Canada)
fax: 812 355 4082

TABLE OF CONTENTS

List of Maps ii

Preface and Acknowledgements iii

Maps

I

Map of Korea showing the Grids and Grid-squares
(Means of reference)

II

Partisan Airborne Operations 1951-1953

II

Overall display of Clandestine Agent/Partisan Operations
1950-1953

Map of Korea depicting Grid Lines and Grid Squares that are used as references to ground locations. Darkened areas show areas of significant Korean Partisan activities, April to July 1953.

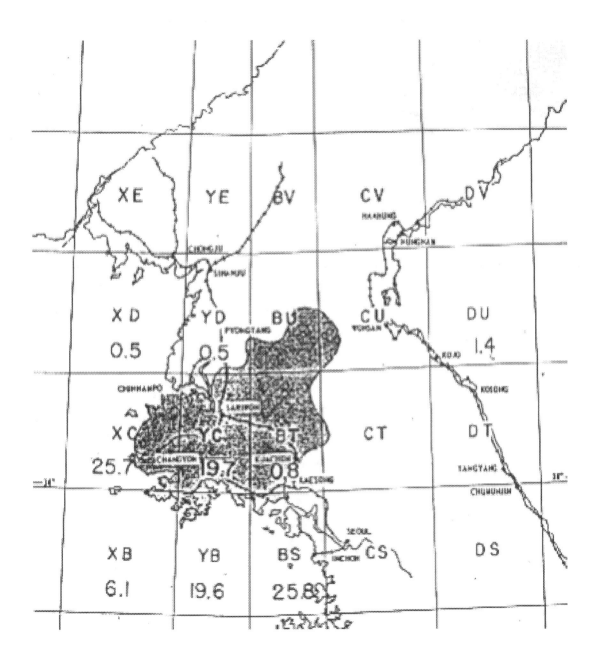

Source: Figure C4. <u>UN Partisan Warfare in Korea, 1951 - 1954</u>, AAFE Group, TM-ORO-T-64, John Hopkins University, 1956, Cleaver, et al.

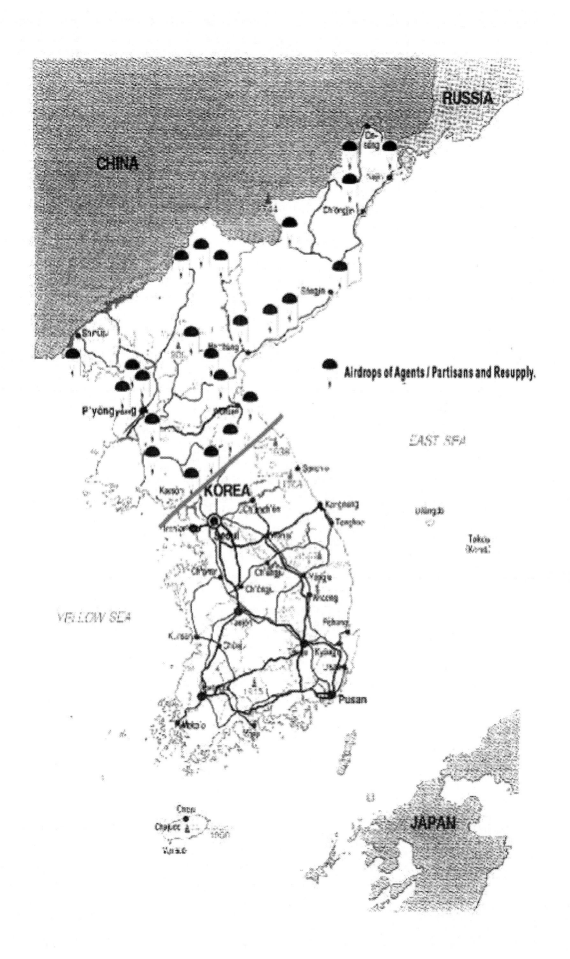

Korean Partisan Unit Dispositions
June 1952

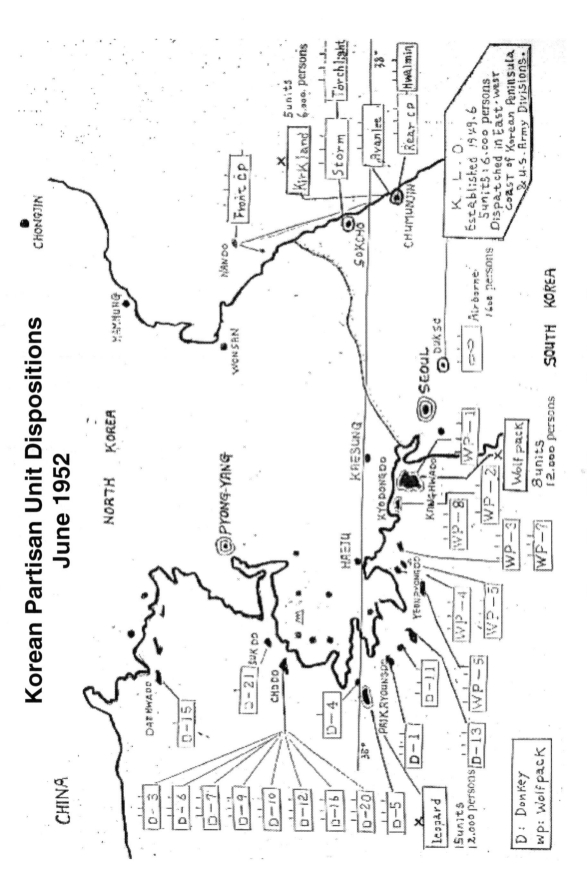

Source: Korean War Commemorative Community
Federation of War Veterans, 8240th, Army Units, Partisan Forces

PREFACE

Ever since I completed my combat tour in Korea in 1952 I have been interested in writing a history of the clandestine airborne operations, especially since I was part of it. However, upon entering the Army Intelligence Corps, I became deeply engaged with classified activities in Europe and naturally avoided revealing even my involvement in such activity during the Korean War knowing these activities were still classified.

After organizing the 8240th Army Unit, 50th Anniversary of the Korean War Commemorative Community in September 2000 and now knowing the secret classifications had been removed, my interest in the subject resurfaced. My feelings were that this unusual activity needed more research and a record made of the heroic efforts of the North Korean anti-Communists is made known to the American public. On the other hand, the courageous acts of the US and British personnel also need to be given the recognition they are certainly due. This book details for the first time the first hand experiences of mine and the personal histories of other veterans who conducted Airborne Special Operations behind the enemy lines. Their stories are fascinating and would be great movie material.

As I began to research the topic, I discovered that many of our US veterans, upon reassignment to the United States, became members of the Special Forces. Most of these were enlisted men and they served in Special Forces for the remainder of their active duty. Many participated in combat operations such as The Dominican Republic, repeated tours in Vietnam, Operations in Panama, Grenada and finally Desert Storm before retirement. This was an unusually devoted, professional group of soldiers who have never received appropriate recognition for their combat service during the Korean War.

In my quest to locate these veterans I had a great opportunity to talk with many of them regarding their Korean combat experiences, especially five AVIARY veterans who served with me in 1952. As my research began I found that many of the descriptions in this article were based on my firsthand knowledge and reinforced by discussions with the AVIARY veterans with whom I either visited or met during the only reunion held in October, 2000, in Panama City Beach, Florida. My trip to Korea earlier that same month also provided information I gathered by discussions with a few of the 350 Korean partisans who attended a luncheon for me. I met again the Donkey 15 leader who was on that bare rocky island when I made the resupply drop in 1952.

I need to recognize the outstanding research efforts of the authors of the fine books that I have referred to in this text and who made a great contribution to the recorded history of the clandestine warfare that was conducted during the Korean War. I want to acknowledge Ed Evenhoe and his book, DARK MOON, Colonel Ben Malcom and his book, WHITE TIGERS, MY SECRET WAR IN NORTH KOREA, and Colonel Mike Haas and his book, IN THE DEVIL'S SHADOW. To them I say thanks for the recorded memories!

I trust my contribution will be regarded as a worthy effort to document details on the specific topic of clandestine airborne operations during the Korean War, their successes, and their failures that influenced the loss of both US, British and patriotic North Korean anti-Communists. All was done in the pursuit of defending the people of the Republic of

South Korea from communist domination.

At this time over fifty years since the end of the Korean War, we have just experienced similar special operations by Special Forces in Afghanistan who carried out almost exactly the same type clandestine airborne operations as covered in this book. Captain Amerine, the Special Forces Commander of the initial Special Forces personnel in Afghanistan, conducted their operation in the same manner as Ranger Sergeant Miles did in 1951 in North Korea. Miles destroyed most of a Chinese Communist Volunteer Army Division with his directed airstrikes using a simple Army radio, where Captain Amerine's troopers utilized state of the art computers, global positioning devices, and radically improved radio equipment.

The results were the same, the destruction of enemy forces. This book details such cases including some tragic losses. The uniqueness of this book is the fact that it reflects the first hand experiences of mine as well as the personal histories of other AVIARY veterans who flew on these dangerous missions, most for an entire year. The book provides details on special operations during the Korean War that are still not generally known. Agent and partisan activity behind enemy lines is movie material. The combined use of American, British, both South and North Koreans and Chinese volunteers in behind the lines combat is unique in itself. The details fill in the missing elements on clandestine airborne operations that other articles and books do not address.

I believe the final chapter of the US Army's use of Homing Pigeons by my unit in Korea is not only an interesting story but also historical in perspective for the US Army.

Generally, the scene is set, as to conditions present that influence the political leaders to make decisions that lead to significant actions, and quite often to hostilities between countries.

My book is set in a wartime period, the Korean War, and the clandestine airborne operations that were conducted. Of course, if one studies the terrain on the Peninsula of Korea, especially the northern portion, it is easy to see the terrain's influence on operations by planners and operational staffs in both BAKER SECTION and AVIARY, the two operational elements that conducted the airborne missions.

From the planner's standpoint, the mountainous terrain offered potentially good sustaining bases for the partisan, while the airborne planners looked for small, reasonably secure drop zones in these mountainous areas. Additionally, both coasts of North Korea also offered a chance for the air dropped team to exfiltrate and be picked-up by off-shore boats that were standing by for their recovery. The other more difficult escape alternative was land exfiltration through both enemy and friendly lines where many agents were inadvertently killed or wounded by friendly forces. The resort to clandestine airborne missions, against targets that were accessible by this method deep inside North Korea, resulted in a great loss of personnel.

A few words need to be devoted to the US personnel who participated in these operations. Some lost their lives, some were critically wounded and disabled for life, some became prisoners of war, while the remainder finished their military careers and also fought several times again before retiring. These men are heroes and deserve great praise for their service that was so closely held as secret until the past few years.

ACKNOWLEDGEMENT
This text is dedicated to honor to these men who served
in Airborne Special Operations

Killed In Action

Army	**Air Force**
Captain David Hern	*Captain Lawrence Burger
Sgt. William T. Miles	
*Cpl. George I. Tatarakis	
*PFC Dean H. Crabb	

* U.S. Army and Airforce personnel killed in action Feb 19 1952 due to
Sabotage by a Chinese double agent of their Aircraft over North Korea.

OTHER PERSONNEL WHO PARTICIPATED
IN AIRBORNE SPECIAL OPERATIONS

Albritton, Emory

Bacera, Francisco

Baker, Raymond E.

Barnes, William

Bayard, Dann

Blimline. William

Bouchardon, Andre

Brewer, Robert

Brooks, David

Carver, Robert, Jr.

Darcy, Paul

Davis, Fred

Dillard, Douglas C.

Forbes, Frank

Garner, Marvin G.

Garvey, William

Green, Lowell

Hagen, Ronald, J.

Hamilton, Ceicil

Harrison, William

Holbert, Chester L.

Hook, Ervin

Jackson, Paul D.

James, Raymond

Joelmore, Kenneth.

Kennedy, James

Kent, William A.

Lancaster, FNU

Leland, George

Lewis, William

Mast, Lester

McCollum, Clarence

Merkls, Robert B.

Nichols-Wells, John

Palmer, Ralph

Panzic, Eckner

Perry, Eugene

Pucel, Edward W.

Romano, Vincent

Slawson, Fred

Sneva, Robert

Staples, Joe

Traynor, Donald

Ulrich, Gerald

Watson, Martin R.

British Army Personnel

Capt. Ellery Anderson, British Army

Lt. Samuel Adams-Acton, British Army
(Killed while trying to escape from the
prisoner of war camp-N. Korea)

Fusilier George Mills, British Army (MIA)

Korean Nationals

Chinese Volunteers

INTRODUCTION

COVERT AIRBORNE OPERATIONS (KOREA)

I was leader of the AVIARY Team of the 8240th Army Unit who had just began recovering from the previous night's flight to drop agents in North Korea, when I received an urgent summons to report to the Guerrilla Operations Section and Major Patterson. Upon arrival, I was briefed on the need to plan for an emergency airdrop of all types of equipment and supplies to the Partisan Team (Donkey 15). This team was now isolated on the small island of Nap-Som-Do just off Tae - Hwado, the northernmost partisan base near the mouth of the Yalu River.

Donkey 15, the partisan unit, had been attacked by the North Korean People's Army forces (NKPA) forces in their efforts to neutralize such partisan bases that supported the partisan operations along the Yalu River as well as monitor activity crossing the river at Sinjuiju into North Korea. Donkey 15 had to conduct an emergency evacuation of the three island bases leaving behind their basic implements of war, their medical supplies, clothing and food. In addition there were several partisans that had been wounded and needed medical care. Essentially, all the personnel of Donkey 15 had left was only the clothes on their backs, and their ANGRC-9 (Angry -9 as referred to by the GIs). Of course the small boats were still sea worthy but, also needed was a supply of fuel to facilitate their movement South to the safehaven of Cho Do (a main partisan island base).

I immediately alerted my deputy, Lt. Emory C. Albritton to begin coordination with Baker Flight of the USAF located at K-16, the airbase near Seoul. While the initial planning for the flight commenced, the logistics personnel of the Guerrilla Operations Section delivered food, medical supplies, ammunition, clothing, and fuel to AVIARY, where the jumpmasters could begin packing for the airdrop.

Communications to support the operation consisted of radio contact between the aircraft and the air coordination center in S. Korea, and naval coordination with ships in the area as well as the radar station on Cho- Do. It should be noted that the timing of the operation was critical to the safety of the Donkey 15 survivors because the NKPA Forces were expected to launch an attack against Nap-Som Island, within the next 24 hours. Nap-Som was about ten miles south of the Chinese occupied island of Tae-Hwa-Do. The proximity to the Chinese and North Korean Coasts presented a threat to surface naval forces operating in that area. The quickest response would be an airdrop with the necessary supplies and equipment to facilitate the evacuation of the island before dawn the following morning. With this threat to the Donkey 15 team uppermost in the minds of the AVIARY personnel, extra efforts were made to complete the necessary coordination of the flight in that area of the combat zone as well as having everything rigged, loaded and second checks made of all matter effecting this resupply operation. This was not a matter of perpetuating on going operations, but to save the lives of the partisans of Donkey 15.

Ground to air communications had to be by basic means. Evidently the radio had malfunctioned so light signals were to be used as a field expedient. The alternative would be for the partisans, upon hearing the aircraft approach at approximately 1AM, they would ignite fires contained in buckets spaced about ten feet apart, and also turn their flashlights skyward, towards the sound of the aircraft and blink them on and off. The AVIARY Jumpmaster would verify the drop zone to the pilot who would then place the aircraft into the drop mode. Essentially such a drop on a very small island with prevailing winds would be difficult at best to hit and this mission required a perfect hit because the resupply could not be redone before morning if the first drop went into the sea!

I directed the loading of the aircraft with Albritton and the crew chief's assistance. Since It was a succeed or fail one time mission the loading became critical because the large load of three containers had to be dropped in tandem, from 500 feet or less on a very small island, drop zone.

To accomplish this drop it was decided to equip the C-47 aircraft floor with the aluminum rollers on which the bundles could be released and pushed on the rollers to the door of the aircraft and one after another jettisoned within seconds. In addition, the bundles were oversized to accommodate the volume of equipment, supplies, and fuel needed by the partisans. To accomplish such a fast drop of the oversized bundles I both the passenger and cargo doors were removed before take off. The pilot was concerned about this facet of the operation due to the drag and extra fuel usage that would be required with an aircraft so configured as well as the distance to be flown. A straight-line course was adopted since most of the flight would be over water with little possibility of ground or antiaircraft fire. The major threat was to enemy aircraft from North Korean or Chinese airfields since the target was within a few flying miles of the Chinese coast. With the aircraft loaded and checked out to the satisfaction of the jumpmaster and the pilot the mission was ready.

The distance from K-16 to the target island was approximately 200 air miles; the flying time to the target was within a two-hour range. Due to the long flight time and the openness of the cargo compartment, the jumpmasters and aircraft crew wore heavy clothing to guard against the extra exposure of the open cargo compartment.

Takeoff was set for 1130 hours, so arrival in the target area would be between 0100-0200 hours. The Donkey 15 commander had been advised of the estimated arrival time so the ground lights would not be ignited for other aircraft, possibly North Korean or Chinese. The takeoff was on schedule and the long flight ensued with frequent position checks by the jumpmaster with the navigator and to move about the aircraft and stimulate the body. Loran was used by the navigator to make constant position checks and also to avoid any conflicts with U. N. naval night intruder flights in the area. Of course there was great apprehension by the crew of being intercepted by a North Korean or Chinese MIG that did frequent the area. The coordination was very important to ensure some protection by UN Aircraft in the area that could respond should a bogey be detected approaching the unarmed C-47 aircraft.

As the aircraft approached the vicinity of the island, the navigator, pilot and jumpmasters discussed again the ground signals to expect. The navigator would advise when the aircraft was in the immediate area of the target and the two jumpmasters, Lt. Albritton and I would begin observing the area for any ground signals. The navigator called on the intercom and advised the pilot and the jumpmaster that the aircraft was in the immediate vicinity of the island and that signals should be seen according to his calculations. What seemed to be an eternity, but only a few minutes in consultation, it was agreed, if the aircraft continued on its current heading it would cross the Chinese coast within a few minutes. A quick agreement was made to continue to fly on the same heading for five minutes then do a 180 degree turn and retrace the flight path on a southerly course. The jumpmaster knowing the importance of helping Donkey 15 survive began a soulful search of his faith for the lights to come on. As the course changed, I requested the pilot, to tap his landing lights on and off, after making his turn, fly at five hundred feet, and to reduce airspeed.

After what seemed to be hours, but in reality a few minutes, the pilot blinked his landing lights twice and just below the aircraft door the first fire on the island came into view. The jumpmaster immediately advised the pilot and requested a rerun over the island in drop mode. By the time the aircraft passed over the island two fires were observed a few feet apart and several flashlights started blinking skyward on each side of the blazing buckets. The illumination from the fires revealed about a dozen figures around the fires with some blinking the flashlights. The jumpmaster's prayers had been answered.[1]

The pilot circled the island and made the same southerly approach as before, the altitude was between 400-500 feet and the plane seemed to slow down as if to make a bus stop. The two jumpmasters assisted by the Crew Chief waited until the aircraft was in level flight and then released the bundle tie downs. The bundles were edged toward the door and as the forward edge of the door lined up with the ground fires, the bundles were salvoed. The altitude was adequate to see the cargo chutes deploy but just briefly before the bundles landed right on line with the ground fires with one bundle actually landing between the ground fires. The partisans on the ground, around the fires could be seen waving thankfully for the resupply. The aircraft made one last circle around the island then headed South to K-16 with no problems, the pilot and navigator did an outstanding job that night finding that needle in the haystack on the Yellow Sea. Weather conditions were not that suitable for such missions, however, since this target drop zone was isolated from land areas and mountainous ranges, the mission could be attempted even through visibility was greatly reduced by overcast skies and drizzling rain. The planners felt their plan was possible because they assumed the island could be located by good navigation, with the low altitude for the drop and ground illumination from the partisan's fires and flashlights it was possible.[2]

The AVIARY Team returned to the 8240th Headquarters to complete its report and debriefing only to learn that the Donkey-15 commander had already sent a message via his ANGRC 9 (with its fresh batteries) to report an excellent airdrop, all supplies recovered, boats refueled and the team would sail to Cho Do before dawn. Needless to say, the AVIARY Jumpmasters were elated to receive confirmation of the successful mission even before being able to report it themselves.[3]

The AVIARY personnel were constantly faced with such life or death missions during the Korean War and they performed in an outstanding manner. These personnel knew each mission north of the Bomb Line in unarmed, slow flying, aircraft was always a great potential target from either enemy aircraft, antiaircraft or ground fire. There was also the ever-present danger of flying into a mountain as they attempted to fly low and slow. This was done to hit drop zones at lower elevations, in small open fields and often located not too far from enemy occupied areas. The foregoing resupply mission illustrates there were very successful covert airborne operations conducted during the Korean War.

In the following descriptive passages an attempt is made to establish the basis for the covert airborne operations, its organization, logistics, personnel and personal stories of these AVIARY veterans for whom I have only the greatest respect and admiration for their repeated outstanding performance in a combat role. Additionally, to record how U. S Army personnel made history in the field of Unconventional Warfare. They provided experience and lessons learned in the subsequent development of Special Forces and its role as a major facet of United States Army Special Operations worldwide.

Author, LT Dillard, Chief, AVIARY, with LT Gardner, USAF Navigator, B-26 aircraft at K-16. Taken early morning after a mission north of Pyongyang, North Korea.

LT Dillard, AVIARY, with C-47 used for clandestine missions over North Korea. Photograph taken at landing strip, Yo Do Island, North Korea.

C-46 aircraft flown by CPT R. Armellino, USAF, on clandestine AVIARY missions over North Korea.

LT Dillard, AVIARY, aboard C-46 aircraft
for a training jump with Korean Partisans,
Aug 52.

LT Dillard on Han River sandbar, Seoul, after jumping
with Leopard Base Partisans.

LT Dillard, AVIARY, on clandestine
mission in North Korea, Feb 52.

CHAPTER I

EVOLUTION OF CLANDESTINE AIRBORNE OPERATIONS (KOREA)

Beginning in late 1950 with the Communist invasion of the Republic of South Korea in progress, the United States Eighth Army recognized the presence of a number of anti-Communist North Korean groups that were engaged in partisan warfare against elements of the North Korean Peoples Army as well as the North Korean Government's Interior Security forces.

It became immediately apparent to the Eighth Army staff that these irregulars, if organized, directed and armed and equipped for extensive ground combat missions, could greatly aid in the defeat of the Communist forces. During the initial stages of this effort, small elite units were organized around the then existing irregular forces. In the beginning, the Miscellaneous Group of the Eighth Army staff started these operations, later becoming the 8086th Army Unit. The basic objectives in employing these irregular forces was to cause disruptions in enemy rear areas, destruction of supplies and material, destroy bridges, make road cuts, block railroad tunnels as well as inflict personnel losses to enemy forces. Such activities in the enemy forces rear areas would therefore, influence the diversion of main force troops to rear area security.[1]

The early stages of development was the initiation off the west coast of North Korea with a partisan base of operations established on the Island of Paengnyong-do from which partisan operations could be effectively supported. This was to become code name William Able. Descriptions of the ground combat activities of these Partisan units are contained in two additional books written by veterans of the Korean supported Special Operations of the 8240th Army Unit. The first is DARK MOON by Ed Evanhoe[2] the second is WHITE TIGERS, MY SECRET WAR IN NORTH KOREA, by Col (Ret) Ben Malcom.[3]

The purpose of this book is to describe the nature of clandestine airborne operations in North Korea during the Korean War. The referenced books do address the detail of some of the operations and difficulties of the clandestine airborne effort, however, they do not address in detail the evolution of the two airborne operational elements, BAKER SECTION and AVIARY, that actually planned and executed the missions.

A succinct description of the clandestine airborne operations is as follows: Indigenous personnel (North and South Koreans and Chinese), often led by US personnel participating in "behind the lines" parachute landings under cover of darkness. Drop zones were located in relatively secure areas, principally mountainous terrain. The intelligence agents collected and reported via radio to UN/US headquarters. Such reported sightings resulted in changes of UN/US troop dispositions as well as in air strikes by UN/US forces against enemy targets that would otherwise not have become known to Eighth Army planners.

The Unites States Airforce supported the clandestine airborne effort with a variety of aircraft that were selected for a particular mission based upon the aircraft's capabilities such as speed, ease of loading and exiting cargo from the aircraft and range. The type of aircraft normally used consisted of the C-47, very good for its normal availability and ease in handling personnel and cargo drops on very small drop zones that required a low and slow flying mode over the drop zone. The C-46, a much larger aircraft with a longer range and the ability to lift heavier loads was used for the long flights into North Korea.

The B26/A-1 Bomber was extremely effective in delivering a limited number of personnel or smaller cargo bundles in areas that had a more effective air defense or the target was near MIG Alley with the potential of attack by enemy fighter aircraft. A limited number of missions were supported with the SA15 aircraft where water landings were necessary. Helicopters, although used effectively to rescue downed airmen was not considered part of the BAKER SECTION or AVIARY operation.[4]

The Airforce initially had difficulty providing experienced pilots with Troop Carrier or other Special Operations backgrounds Detailed in this book are some of the problems that were encountered in conducting the clandestine airborne effort.

I am still in contact with one of the pilots with whom I flew many of these missions. He has detailed his experiences and his background under chapter VIII personal histories in this book. One must also take into account that the Special Operations concept, as recognized today, was not of particular interest to planners who were suddenly confronted with fielding a fighting force to engage in a main force land battle on the Korean Peninsular, similar to the Italian Campaign of W.W.II. So the thought of diverting any resources to an unconventional warfare effort, at least in the initial stages of the war was not very attractive. Simply stated, the effort had to come from in Theater resources. The Airforce provided aircraft and crews on temporary duty (TDY) from Japan. which required a constant reorientation of pilots in this kind of clandestine airborne activities. On February 19, 1952, a C-46 aircraft with both Korean and Chinese irregulars aboard, three personnel from the 8240th Army Unit (Army Jumpmasters) and two aircrews, one experienced crew and a new TDY crew, were lost when the aircraft was sabotaged by one of the agents. More detail follows about actual Airborne Operations. The point is, not withstanding the loss of the agents and the jumpmaster; two crews were also lost![5]

The BAKER SECTION AND AVIARY were comprised principally, of US Army personnel, except at the beginning of operations in 1951. At this time the airborne effort under BAKER SECTION conducted several operations with British personnel. In 1951, under Colonel McGee's leadership the Baker Section materialized with a concept of airborne operations to be US/British lead and to establish irregular force bases in North Korea to sustain operations over an extended period of time. Since these bases would be located in isolated areas the clandestine airborne effort would be needed to communicate and resupply the bases. The actual first airdrop by the Baker Section was on March 15, 1951, on the target drop zone Hyon-ni, in North Korea. From that time until the end of hostilities in 1953 clandestine airborne operations continued with such operations ranging from the drop of one agent to respectively, large guerrilla teams, radio intercepts and resupply.[6]

The initial clandestine airborne operation VIRGINIA I experienced great difficulties with both the airdrop and with its ground actions. Subsequently the second operations code name SPITFIRE was launched at 2030 hours, June 18, 1951. Its drop zone southeast of Karyoju-Ri, North Korea, was to be followed up with three additional drops to buildup the personnel strength at the base. The second drop was June 26,1951. The British officer Lt. Adams-Acton damaged his knee during the drop, which later had an impact on the ground operations. With so much difficulty with this second mission, the Headquarters staff was quite upset with its failure. On July 13/14 1951, the experienced Capt. David Hearn accompanied by a Korean interpreter jumped in the area carrying a PRC-10 with extra batteries (the thought being that should communication be reestablished the operation perhaps could continue). However, it became necessary for the entire team to exfiltrate through friendly lines. Each of these airborne operations is described in greater detail in Chapter VI, Selected Clandestine Airborne Operations.[7]

Up to this time the Clandestine Airborne effort had been controlled by BAKER SECTION. The reality being it was more than a training and air delivery operations but also engaged its personnel in participating in the behind the lines drops. There had been an initial contest of wills among the Miscellaneous Group staffs over Captain Hearn's participation, due to his detail knowledge of all agent operations by the Miscellaneous Group. It seemed that in desperation over the failure of the SPITFIRE operations, Captain Hearn was still permitted to jump into the area, in an attempt to salvage the operation. Captain Hearn was knowledgeable of the entire airborne activity and its personnel so his capture on this mission could have resulted in its compromise assuming his torture during interrogation would have forced him to talk.[8]

At about this time Colonel McGee, the Chief of the Miscellaneous Group was preparing to rotate from Korea and his successor Lt. Col. Samuel Koster, his Executive, was to assume control. Additionally, pressure from both Eighth Army and the Far East Command began to rise as well as demand that the Unconditional Warfare activities be organized under an overall control and coordinating headquarters. In the case of the clandestine airborne operations effort something needed to be done to improve the operations.

After an evaluation of the actions of the pilot on the SPITFIRE operation and the discovery that cargo chutes did not deploy due to incorrect rigger procedures, the US Army addressed its failures, while the USAF also made many changes. It reorganized by activating a Special Missions Squadron and directed extensive training for its aircrews in pinpointing drop zones, as well as developing expertise in conducting night time airdrops that would also require evasive flying in large, unarmed, slow flying aircraft into hot drop zones in unfamiliar territory. The USAF unit was located at the Atsugi Air Base, Japan. Additionally, USAF liaison personnel attached to US Army Operational headquarters and US Eighth Army, promoted enhancement of such operations in the future.[9]

Earlier in the year, March 1951, as a result of the compromise of a North Korean Spy ring in the Pusan area, the Commands became more concerned about security. Since the BAKER SECTION operations had been penetrated, a need to reorganize the effort proceeded. The overall control and coordinating headquarters, the Combined Command for Reconnaissance Activities (Korea), decided the issue of the clandestine airborne activities by organizing a new Airborne staff and operational element under its control. The BAKER SECTION functions then became dormant, while the new entity code name AVIARY from its humble beginning in August 1950, near Pusan greatly expanded.

Initially, AVIARY conducted airborne training, practice jumps and the delivery of the agents and their resupply. Although, the partisan airborne operations essentially stopped after the SPITFIRE OPERATION, they started again in February 1952 with a drop of a partisan team north of Pyongyang, on the Southern end of MIG Alley. Thus, the complete change over of all clandestine airborne activities became the province of

AVIARY.[10]

An excellent narrative that details the initiation of Clandestine Airborne operations in Korea is contained in Warren A. Trest's book, Air Commando One, Heine Aderholt and America's Secret Air Wars. The narrative is based upon interviews with BG. Aderholt (r) USAF, who was instrumental in developing the Airforce supporting activities for Col. Brewer (r) US Army who conducted clandestine collection operations in response to collection requirements of the Far East Command and the US Eighth Army. Aderholt explains meeting Brewer in October 1950 and Brewers request for air support in dropping agents in North Korea and resupplying them afterwards. Aderholt readily agreed to provide the support and over the next ten months, they mutually developed procedures for the clandestine airborne effort. Brewer states that over the ten-month period they conducted an average of about twenty missions per month. In this period Brewer claims approximately one thousand agents were dropped throughout North Korea and approximately 70% returned to friendly lines.[11] General Aderholt help develop an improved air ground communications procedure with the use of a long coaxial trailing antenna behind the aircraft that improved the capability to communicate with agents on the ground within a ten mile radius. These initial clandestine airborne operations were principally to collect information of a tactical nature, many of short duration by the agent operating behind the lines. It should be noted records show that clandestine airborne operations were conducted beginning in August 1950, however Brewer experienced more difficulty in obtaining aircrews experienced in flying these nighttime, low altitude flights over North Korea in unarmed, slow flying aircraft. Additionally, once the crews knew what the mission entailed they were not very happy in executing them. With General Aderholt Brewer found a stouthearted pilot ready to take on the challenge.[12]

Beginning in January 1951 the nature of the operations began to change with expanding numbers of operations that were initiated by intelligence collection requirements of the Far East Command, the US Eighth Army, the US 5th Airforce and the CIA. From this hastily organized effort developed mutually by BG Aderholt for the Airforce and Col. Brewer for the Army, the clandestine airborne operations became AVIARY under the control of the Far East Command Liaison Detachment (FECLD). General Aderholt and Colonel Brewer rotated from Korea and subsequently were detailed to duty with the CIA. These two individuals under the pressure of contributing to the combat effort through their ingenuity, dedication to duty and perseverance with their own services established the base for the clandestine airborne effort that continued through out the remaining years of combat.

CHAPTER II

STRATEGY AND TECHNIQUES OF AERIAL DELIVERY

I followed the accepted techniques experienced during World War II and subsequent airborne training exercises conducted in peacetime, prior to the beginning of the Korean War. In the interim between wars, the military services suffered shortfalls in funding for training purposes, and while the US Army airborne forces namely the Parachute School at Fort Benning, Georgia produced fewer graduates, for the 82d Airborne Division, planes to drop troopers were in short supply as well.

Many exercises were simulated airborne drops, followed by the usual ground exercise. From the beginning of 1947 until the outbreak of hostilities in Korea, the most available source of aircraft was a single C-47 plane that was assigned to the US Airforce Liaison Officer attached to the Division. This aircraft was used constantly for "pay jumps." In 1946, due to a number of troopers refusing to make a jump onto an uncleared Drop Zone at Fort Bragg, NC, an administrative requirement was promulgated that required quarterly pay jumps in order to draw jump pay.

Actual airborne exercises and the Pathfinder and Jumpmaster training courses were constrained by the number of courses that could be run as well as the size of the classes. When US Airforce aircraft was available there was an intense effort to maximize their use in the conduct of unit airborne exercises. As the Korean War began so did an intensive effort to bring up the airborne forces to acceptable readiness levels. The 187th Airborne Regimental Combat Team was assembled at Fort Campbell, Kentucky for deployment to Korea and the Airborne Infantry Rangers Companies began organizing and training at Fort Benning, Georgia. So in the summer of 1950 the airborne forces of the United States gained the resources needed to once again become proficient in conducting airborne operations.[1]

The foregoing information is important for the reader to understand the actual readiness of these airborne forces at the beginning of the Korean War. One can readily see the shortages that existed in men, equipment, material, as well as the availability of constant, intensive airborne training exercises needed to maintain readiness for deployment.

I would discover that the staff of the AVIARY team generally followed the basics of parachute landing techniques in the training of clandestine agents and partisans. I made a determined effort to review these basics with the staff and insisted they be followed.

The application of these techniques would make the difference in the initial survival of an agent or guerrilla as well as their ability to locate aerial delivery containers dropped with them. Essentially, if the Jumpmaster had done his homework conscientiously, the agent or partisan then had to successfully apply what he had learned in training to control his chute and make a proper parachute landing.

When tasked by the 8240th Staff for a mission, the AVIARY jumpmaster who would conduct the airdrop, then completed the following coordinations:

Evaluation of the mission requirements such as number of indigenous personnel and aerial delivery containers needed, coordination with the indigenous team handler to acquire the items to be dropped, any special escort requirements by the agents team or a guerrilla unit representative. Quite often an alternative drop zone was needed as a diversion. Someone must then brief the agents or partisans on the change; therefore, the language problem would necessitate an additional passenger aboard for the mission. With the C-47and C-46 this was not a problem, but the B-26 Bombers provided very limited space in its bomb bay, therefore, an additional person would not be taken.[2]

A very thorough map reconnaissance and review of available aerial photographs of the target area was necessary to select the best possible drop zone. Such facets of selecting the shortest route to the drop zone, areas that avoided concentrations of antiaircraft gun positions, and likely aircraft warning posts were very important. The use of the defilade of mountains and/or hills to facilitate surprise as well as providing distinctive features along the route that aid in navigation were absolutely essential to the success of any clandestine airborne mission. Actual aerial reconnaissance of the target drop zone usually could not be done for fear of compromising the mission.

The joint coordination with the pilot and navigator was essential to success. For example, the altitude of flight during the approach should be low unless the drop zone is hard to find. A low approach enhances surprise since the aircraft cannot be seen from any distance. Furthermore a low flying aircraft is more difficult for fighter aircraft to attack, or for antiaircraft to hit, except for small arms fire. (Many of the AVIARY mission aircraft experienced numerous hits from this source, usually from the vicinity of the drop zone)

The main disadvantage of the low approach is that navigation is difficult, drop zones are hard to locate and or fly over properly, unless distinctive landmarks are present. The fact that aerial reconnaissance usually could not be made, the coordination in the jumpmaster, pilot, navigator conference would determine the final method of drop to be conducted. Without the reconnaissance of the area, the high approach over the drop zone normally should be made along the axis of the drop zone and from the direction of the approach. Additionally, the altitude of the jump would depend upon the size of the drop zone (to ensure hitting the smaller drop zones) as well as the likelihood of enemy or security forces being in close proximity to the drop zone.[3]

For the safety of the jumper, personnel drops were not considered below 500 feet. Each jumpmaster and the pilot had to keep in mind, especially with C-47 and C-46 type aircraft that, assuming the transport type aircraft can slow its speed to about 90-100 miles per hour, the aircraft often will lose about 200 feet of altitude while in this jump mode. Therefore, it was exceedingly important for the pilot and navigator, along with the jumpmaster to carefully compute the effect of the terrain versus the drop zone and altitude to be used for the drop in order to successfully make the drop and clear the terrain obstacles in the immediate area,

During the in-bound flight, the jumpmaster maintains a constant vigilance from the open door of the aircraft to maintain an awareness of distinguishing landmarks along the flight route, and especially as the aircraft approaches the vicinity of the drop zone. The jumpmaster always attempts to verify the position near the drop zone and specifically identify the drop zone as best he can depending upon the drop zone visibility. The jumpmaster had to constantly converse with the pilot and navigator during the flight. The pilot often can gauge the effect or estimate of the wind by its effect on the aircraft, which also influences the drop. If the crew and jumpmaster feel there is a tail wind of an appreciable amount the drop would commence on the rear edge of the drop zone, the same applies for a head wind, so the drop begins about 200 yards past the near edge of the drop zone. In case there is no feeling for wind on the drop zone the drop should commence about 100 yards into the drop zone. Usually, the pilot who has sensed any cross wind would compensate for it by flying left or right of the center of the drop zone. If there were no concern for a crosswind, the aircraft would fly across the center of the drop zone. The changes of approach the pilot felt he must make would be relayed to the jumpmaster so he was aware of where over the drop zone he should commence the drop.[4]

During the analysis of the failures in the airdrop portion of the earlier clandestine airborne operations, it was generally accepted that the following frequent shortfalls in jumpmaster, pilot and navigator inexperience occurred:

* Insufficient study of maps and aerial photographs before mission planning.
* Faulty scheduling that results in the scheduled drop or the agents/guerrillas not in position to execute
* Frequency of aircraft in the vicinity of the drop zone for 2nd phase drops, resupply or radio intercepts that compromised the drop zone to enemy military or security
* Incomplete briefing of agents/guerrillas on exiting aircraft promptly, or controlling parachute during descent or improper parachute landing fall, resulting in injury
*Lack of attention to detail in the inspection of all equipment from the personnel parachute to every item to be carried on the mission resulted in parachute malfunction, loss of equipment and/or failure to bring all equipment specified. The AVIARY team was responsible for all items of airborne equipment and the secure and safe rigging of the aerial delivery containers. The agent handler or partisan unit sponsor was responsible for providing the other operational equipment need to conduct the operation. For example, on a short penetration mission in the summer of 1952, I conducted an intelligence agent team drop in the vicinity of Wonsan, North Korea. The team was given two sets of pigeons; each set on a different agent to ensure the survival of at least one set. The agents upon landing released the first set of pigeons before daybreak with a capsule message showing they landed safely on the correct drop zone and had recovered their equipment. The morning of the second day, the other set of pigeons were released that carried a message indicating the agents had reached their operating base and would begin collection operations. After the arrival of the pigeons, no further contact was made with the team. About a week later the team members exfiltrated through the lines in the X Corps sector and were recovered by an 8240th Tactical Liaison Team.[5] Upon being debriefed it was learned that the agent handler for that team had failed to provide to the team the crystals needed to operate the ANGRC-9 radio. This incident, of course, caused lots of concern within the Headquarters and brought forth more checks among the teams for all items of equipment needed to conduct the operation.
* Confusion during preparation to load the aircraft causing more tension among the indigenous agents or partisans and their confidence in the jumpmaster.
* Jumpmasters too eager, jumping the personnel too soon and perhaps dropping the so that is landed away from the drop zone.
* Pilots failing to fly the agreed course properly and failing to compensate for cross wind, thereby influencing the jumpmaster to miscalculate his drop accurately.

* Agents/partisans failing to locate their own equipment chutes in the air, resulting in delay or loss of the equipment. Additionally, danger of being discovered by security forces. The foregoing areas of failure crippled an unknown number of missions, in spite of exerted efforts to properly train the indigenous personnel for the airborne portion of his or her mission. Although there was a need to know about the operation itself, agreement was reached to brief the AVIARY team after each mission so any shortfalls in airborne training or delivery could be corrected.[6]

For resupply drops the same basics were employed to drop on target. However, to avoid compromise of the operational area, resupply drop zones were to locate away from the operational site and changed with each resupply drop. Ground signals of various types, including radio signals were employed. Agents using flashlights in a circle or square formation could be so identified from the aircraft. Controlled signal fires that were very prominently used, in conjunction with flashlights, worked well with partisan units on the islands, but inland, many wood fires caused by fire farmers or lightning strikes often masked the signal fire of the agent. The mission would have to be rescheduled thereby causing more ground activity to locate a new drop zone as well as the more frequent presence of troop carrier type aircraft flying in the area, that no doubt compromised some operations to enemy security.

The next area of concern was the proper rigging of the aircraft for the personnel drops as well as cargo drops. On C-46 and C-47 type aircraft, depending upon the load, only the passenger door was used and the necessary masking tape applied to rough edges. In some instances as indicated earlier in this article, the entire cargo door was removed to facilitate salvoing the cargo bundles over very small drop zones, immediately upon the last agent exiting the aircraft. The indigenous jumpers were trained to begin searching the sky around them for their bundles, after their own parachute had deployed. During the briefing of the personnel, they were told exactly when their bundles would be dropped and about where on the drop zone they should look for them. After landing, if they detected a strong ground wind they then had to determine in what direction their bundles would drift. As a general rule the actual dropping of indigenous personnel was not a problem if the basics were followed by the jumpmaster and the pilot maintained the agreed upon approach and altitude across the drop zone. In the event, the jumpmaster detected small arms fire from the vicinity of the drop zone he would abort the mission by stopping the jump and immediately notifying the pilot to depart the area. This detection was very easy due to the flash of weapons being fired on the ground and on some occasions the odor of fuel leaking from penetrations of small arms fire into the wings of the aircraft. This happened more times than the AVIARY veterans like to remember. In rigging the aircraft, on occasion, after receiving the Airforce briefing of a hot target, the place crew along with AVIARY personnel would spread Flak Pads on the floor of the aircraft in anticipation of taking small arms hits.[8]

The use of the B-26 or A1 as some like to refer to this bomber presented a different approach in its rigging for both personnel and aerial delivery container drops. First, the Bombay provided very limited space for personnel. Not more than three agents or two agents and a jumpmaster could be seated on a narrow wooden board seat that had been made by the aircraft maintenance crew at K-16. This narrow seat was hung by metal hooks to the bomb shackles within the Bombay and secured to the inboard side of the Bombay. The personnel in the Bombay were seated with their legs dangling below the

Bombay doors. As the door closed, their legs were raised on the inside of the doors and they remained seated and already hooked up for the drop. [9]

The senior jumpmaster, normally would seat himself alongside the navigator in the nose of the B-26 or the plastic bubble (soft nosed B-26). From that location both the jumpmaster and navigator had an excellent view of the terrain and could instantly agree on the landmarks as well as verify the drop zone. The jumpmaster riding in the Bombay with the indigenous personnel could talk to the jumpmaster over the intercom and receive instructions for the drop as well as the actual command to execute. The space limitations in the B-26 almost cost the life of Corporal Carver on his last mission. With agents in the Bombay and Carver monitoring them from the jumpseat where there is also a small opening from which one can reach into the Bombay, the mission proceeded to the area just north of the Bomb Line to dispatch the agents on a tactical intelligence collection mission. As the aircraft let down to drop altitude it was hit by heavy antiaircraft machine gun fire. As luck would have it, the armor plating on the B-26 had one small area on its fuselage, where the receding cover for a ladder to drop down so the crew can climb up into the cockpit, was not armor plated. The rounds entered that spot passed up through Carver's Right knee and right hand then passed out the top of the cockpit just above the head of the pilot. Due to the cramped space, the co-pilot could not turn around to administer first aid, so the navigator crawled through the tunnel from the nose of the aircraft, leaned over the co-pilot and tried to place a tourniquet on Carver's leg. Meanwhile, the pilot aborted the mission and radioed K-9, Kimpo Airfield, to foam the runway since they did not know of possible other hits on the bomber. Even after landing it took considerable time for the medics to rig a gurney on a sling to lift Carver from the cockpit. He had suffered a considerable loss of blood, but did survive and was retired with disability. The three agents in the Bombay were covered with Carver's blood as the air stream carried it directly into the Bombay area. Needless to say that ended their fervor for anymore airborne missions. [10]

The use of SA-16 Seaplanes was limited but utilized where a water landing was necessary to either dispatch an agent who subsequently made a water infiltration or reversed the process and was picked up after exfiltrating by boat from the target area. [11]

Resupply drops from the B-26 also were limited by space in number and size of the containers. Usually, the jumpmaster would rig the bundles by placing them on a wooden platform that was anchored to the bomb shackles, with the jumpmaster also sitting on the platform. He was equipped with an intercom system and maintained a dialogue with the pilot and navigator throughout the mission. The altitude for the drop was always attempted at the lowest level possible which was consistent with the air defense environment, the type of terrain along the route of approach and the size of the drop zone. Usually, the B-26 resupply missions required only one bundle, or perhaps two small bundles, depending upon their contents and concern to not mix hard objects such as weapons, ammunition with radios, radio parts, liquid medicines or other items that could be more easily damaged.

With AVIARY and the operational teams concerned with the foregoing, the US Airforce was faced with enhancing the operational environment of its aircraft. The troop carrier type aircraft had to be modified to cope with the nighttime, classified missions over unfamiliar terrain presenting a potential target for every armed combatant. To this end, the aircraft that still carried the flat-silver finish were painted an olive drab color.

Although the C-47, I used in 1952, never changed its color, rather its underbelly was painted black. Further engine exhaust extensions that reduced visibility of the low-lying aircraft were installed to reduce its visibility to the ground observer. As already mentioned the addition of the flak pads for floor cover helped morale of the aircrews and jumpmasters as well.[12]

As in all type operations, communications although extremely important seem to lag behind in development. In this instance, the use of the long drag antennae behind the aircraft improved the system and the availability of the US Army SCR 300 Radio Set. This radio was in great demand by the front-line Infantry units and required a high priority to acquire for the Unconventional Warfare effort. As they became more available, all elements of the Clandestine Special Operations effort improved. The ability to communicate with the friendly agents or partisan units on the ground for a recovery or resupply greatly improved. In many instances the capability aided in advising the friendly elements of security forces or other order of battle information that became available to the 8240th Army Unit and needed to be communicated to these behind the lines elements to avoid their compromise. The greatest improvement came with the availability of the PRC-10 radio that was much lighter, had a longer battery life, and was frequently modulated (FM). This one advantage greatly aided operations since the CCF and NKPA forces could not monitor FM radio transmissions. Obviously the initial demand by all US units limited the availability of the PRC 10s.

The AN/GRC-9 Radio was the principal radio issued to the agents or partisans for communications with the Headquarters. It could be powered by battery or by use of a hand crank. As a matter of fact, the partisan teams started calling themselves DONKEYS because they felt they resembled a donkey while using the handcrank to power the ANGRC-9. Subsequently the partisan units adopted the term- donkey- and each guerrilla team became a code numbered donkey unit.

I flew many of these missions with Captain Richard Armellino, a C-46 pilot who flew 200 missions in support of the clandestine airborne effort. He points out the AVIARY jumpmasters became more than a team, they became an intregal part of a unified mission concept. Here is how Armellino describes the strategy employed in these missions. "On most night missions my jumpmasters were Dillard and Albritton. These were obviously very well trained and professional soldiers. They showed extreme concern for our jumpers. Their strategies are indelible in my mind even after almost 50 years. One great idea was to always fly well north of our target so that we'd be on a southerly heading into the target area to avoid listening devices and radar as much as possible. The Chinese would not expect aircraft well north of any combat zones.

Second strategy was to drop from under 800 to 1000 feet in the mountains so that the hang time was as little as possible; also drop heading across the valley and limit fire from the MSR's. A third strategy was to locate the drop zone, proceed 1-20 miles past, then circle a few times and proceed to the target and drop.

After all of this we would place 30 caliber machine guns against the drop doorframes and fire at anything or nothing. All of this was done to protect our troopers the best way we knew. The coup de grace were fake bombs in the form of GI gas cans dropped with phosphorus bombs attached-giving the appearance of a small A-bomb at 3 a.m. on a dark night." The entire letter is included in chapter VIII, personal histories in this book.

Captain Armellino further describes some techniques he used as follows; "Flying in the mountains on a dark moonless night required some different techniques. We would use a number of one-piece 3 dimensional plastic maps. I guess about 30 inches square-2 inches high. The sectors were lettered from left to right, from south to north, west to east; left bottom was AA, AB, AC and so on. The row above was BA, BB, BC and so on. The lettered squares were 1" square and each inch was 6 miles.

By flying at 180 miles per hour, I could follow a string -knotted every inch. We held the string across the map with scotch tape. One night flying trick was to let down below the mountaintops while over the east coast, ocean or a large lake. That would silhouette the mountains even on the darkest night. There was a large lake in North Korea that I used quite often for that purpose. I was also under the impression that to fly with the engines out of sync could confuse the listening devices or radar."

The foregoing review of strategies and techniques is designed to familiarize the reader with several aspects of airborne operations. One aspect is the accepted airborne doctrine based on World War II experience. Another aspect is the unique applications of air delivery of personnel, equipment and resupply necessary to support the clandestine airborne operations of the Korean War.

Korean AVIARY Instructor, Byon Youn Duk, jumping on to the Han River sandbar, Aug 52.

LT Emory Albritton, Assistant AVIARY Trainer, jumps on to the Han River sandbar, Aug 52.

Byon Youn Duk, Korean AVIARY Instructor, descends on to the Han River sandbar, Aug 52.

Drop zone for training Agents and Partisans, Seoul, Korea.

Alsom Island off Wonson Harbor. Partisan Base with no adequate drop zone. Resupply drops had to be a pinpoint drop into the Compound.

Yo Do Island, West Coast Partisan Base.

Yo Do Island, off west coast of North Korea. Partisan Base with short landing strip. AVIARY made resupply drops when landings were not possible.

CHAPTER III

PERSONNEL STAFFING

Various studies and articles that have been written about the operations of the differing combat elements of the unconventional warfare activities of the 8240th Army Unit. None have been more critical than those comments regarding the clandestine airborne element during the Korean War.

In the beginning of this book I attempted to demonstrate operations that, in fact, saved the partisans of Donkey 15 from potential annihilation. The cited operation was only one of many such radio contacts or resupply activities that facilitated continuation of the intelligence collection or partisan attacks against the enemy forces and infrastructure in their own rear areas. It is felt important to lead into the facets of obtaining qualified airborne experienced personnel to conduct training and make pinpoint airdrops as well as developing a system of logistic support for quartermaster items of airborne delivery of gear and equipment to support the effort. Although clandestine airborne operations were conducted early in the Korean War, the scale of airborne operations began to rise in volume beginning in February 1952 on a scale that necessitated the development of an infrastructure. This infrastructure provided both personnel and material on a much more demanding scale than previously with the BAKER SECTION operations.[1]

Colonel McGee established the clandestine airborne effort under operation code name BAKER SECTION. Additionally, BAKER SECTION assumed control of the existing Ranger Training School located at Kijang, fifteen miles northeast of Pusan. The Ranger School's staff were absorbed into BAKER SECTION, since the school cadre offered qualified airborne staff with their Ranger associated field experience. The facility provided for the construction of the usual 34-foot towers and platforms for practicing parachute-landing falls.[2]

The operational airborne element, the Eighth Army Aerial Delivery and Communications Detachment, located at airbase K-3 near Pusan performed the actual personnel and resupply airdrops with the indigenous personnel graduates of the old Ranger School. In addition, the detachment also air dropped Eighth Army and Far East Command agents in North Korea. This same support was provided on occasion to the CIA operational element in Korea. A separate compartmented airborne element was also located in Pusan, the Eighth Army Liaison Office for Oceanic Research, was established under the leadership of Captain Ellery Anderson, a British Officer, who had served in the British Special Air Service (SAS). This element was essentially a school for sabotage activities specializing in demolitions. These elements then constituted the beginning of a more organized effort to expand clandestine airborne operations in support of the UN forces.

The Eighth Army Miscellaneous Group staff had personnel who were airborne qualified and some with World War II combat experience, such as Captain David Hearn who, as an enlisted man had worked with the OSS and jumped behind Japanese lines in China. There was a Major Eugene Perry who initially commanded BAKER SECTION, and had special operations experience. For the first operation that was to be US led, the need for qualified and combat experience enlisted men became apparent. The most readily available source of airborne qualified, combat experienced men was the Airborne Ranger Companies that were attached to each US front-line division. Four Rangers were selected from the 4th Ranger Company to participate in VIRGINIA I, the forthcoming clandestine airborne operation. They were Corporals Martin Watson, Edward Pucel, William T. Miles, and Pfc. Raymond E. Baker. Pucel, a veteran of the OSS in Europe and the rest were combat veterans of W.W.II. All of these Rangers participated in the VIRGINIA I operation.[3]

The VIRGINIA I operation coupled with the failure of the SPITFIRE operation that was conducted in June 1951, as alluded to earlier in this article essentially stalled further unit operations of this type. Until the beginning of 1952 when the next such type operation was executed in February 1952. During this hiatus in BAKER SECTION operations, planning was on going to reorganize the overall effort and expand the scale of operations. A failure of cargo chutes to deploy during the SPITFIRE operation and the suspected penetration of BAKER SECTION by a North Korean spy ring did influence the wholesale transfer of the clandestine airborne operations. The operations were transferred to the newly expanded AVIARY team, controlled by the Far East Command Liaison Detachment that was an element reporting to the Far East Command.

After examining the weaknesses of BAKER SECTION it is important to review weaknesses in the early stages of the AVIARY operations. Essentially designed to train and airdrop agents for intelligence collection purposes, the AVIARY effort was also plagued with some of its own problems. Recovered agents from airdrops, upon debriefing provided the clues to mission failures in AVIARY operations. For example, the agents stated they had not received any training in parachuting until the day of the mission. The limited training consisted of how to fit the chute to their body size, hookup the static line in the aircraft and exiting the door. There was no practice of parachute landing falls or how to manipulate the chute during their descent; essentially no instruction was given on the basics of parachute jumping. Further, it was discovered that the officer jumpmaster normally was forward with the pilot and navigator during the drops and relied upon the enlisted assistant jumpmaster to conduct the actual jump. Stated most often, was they did not land anywhere near their drop zone and the maps provided to them by the agent team handler were old and without any ground navigation training (map reading), making the maps useless. With this knowledge, the AVIARY team was reorganized and staffed with a group of qualified airborne enlisted men from the personnel pipeline at Camp Drake. Japan. The AVIARY officer responsible for these failures was relieved. Thus began the orderly expansion of the clandestine airborne effort.[4]

While this recent analysis of the clandestine airborne operations influenced changes in AVIARY, it also impacted on the US Airforce pilots and navigators who were providing the air support. The Fifth Airforce staff immediately ordered extensive troop carrier training for the aircrews in Japan to enhance their skills in navigation and pinpoint locations of small drop zones in unfamiliar territory often within mountainous ranges and the ability to successfully operate during nighttime. Aircrews were rotated between Japan and Korea on a thirty-day basis. As alluded to in his written observations, former Airforce Captain Richard Armellino, a C-46 pilot, recalled to active duty from the USAF Air Reserves in New York State, describes his experiences with AVIARY. He volunteered to serve an extended period in Korea, to earn the 1 point per mission, thereby expediting his eligibility for early rotation. Captain Armellino flew 200 missions during the summer months of 1952. Fortunately for AVIARY, Captain Armellino had extensive experience in the C-46, had trained with General Singlaub at Fort Benning, Georgia with the Rangers and also had extensive flying experience in Japan and Korea in 1951 before beginning his tour with the clandestine airborne effort. This pilot was one of the very few who had the experience needed by the effort[5]

When missions in hot spots well defended by antiaircraft were necessary, AVIARY resorted to the use of B-26 bombers. Their speed, long range and a capability to defend themselves were assets to the effort, but space in the bomb bay limited the number of agents that could be carried and limited space for aerial delivery containers. When more than two agents were aboard they were required to carry supplies directly on their person or in small field packs attached to their parachute harness. On resupply missions with only cargo, again the number and size of the containers were restricted. The main point here is that a constant change in pilots and navigators hindered the success of some missions due to missed drop zones or delayed signals to make the drop. There were two exceptions with B-26 pilots. Captain Van Fleet (son of the Eighth Army Commander) and Captain Black who did make repeated missions that improved in efficiency with each mission. Sadly, Captain Van Fleet was lost on a regular night intruder mission in his B-26.[6]

The analysis completed by the G-2, Far East Command and in conjunction with the US Eighth Army, efforts were exerted to improve personnel procurement and straighten the logistical chain of support. For the AVIARY team this meant recommending a procedure to identify qualified airborne personnel, preferably with combat experience as they arrived in the personnel pipeline in Japan. Additionally, a procedure was necessary to conduct personal interviews in Japan and to also reject personnel who did not pass the screening for such classified duties. The Far East Command provided the Replacement Center at Camp Drake with the qualifications for assignment to the classified program, however, the personnel screening (interviews) would be conducted by a representative of the Far East Command Liaison Group in Tokyo.

My personal experience illustrates this new procedure. Only after I arrived at Camp Drake in January 1952 did I learn of the need for volunteers for a classified program. This new organization was being formed in Korea with airborne qualified, combat experienced infantry officers. Both Lt. Albritton and were placed on hold at Camp Drake pending an interview. Within days we were escorted to the Headquarters of the Far East Command Liaison Group and interviewed. Even during the interview no details of actual duty assignment was revealed. A picture of an adventurous assignment in Korea, working on a secret project that was directly under General McArthur's Intelligence staff was presented. After responding to many questions regarding my combat record as well as my extensive airborne experience, the interviewer stated the we were accepted and would be called in for a few days of temporary duty with the headquarters for detailed briefings. After the temporary duty was completed, we were issued clothing, equipment, a 45-caliber pistol, and then flown to K-16, Korea. As it turned out, Lt. Albritton became my assistant AVIARY officer. After we completed the orientations in Japan we were flown together to Korea.[7]

Enlisted personnel records were screened at the replacement center and they were processed in a similar manner. However, on occasion, some made the trip to Korea via troop ship and then joined the AVIARY Team. During this reorganization and expansion of the effort, in-country resources were also available to the AVIARY TEAM. The only airborne units in Korea were the Airborne Infantry Ranger Companies that were deactivated in September 1951, therefore, making available several hundred outstanding combat personnel. A great number of these Rangers joined the 8240th Army Unit, while the majority joined the many Partisan Infantry Regiments of the partisan effort and a few were assigned to AVIARY. The team was comprised of two officers and at times varying numbers of enlisted men. Due to rotation of personnel, the increasing number of missions and the availability of a number of qualified enlisted personnel assigned throughout the organization, occasional reinforcement of the AVIARY activity occurred. In 1952, while I headed AVIARY, the enlisted complement was approximately twelve jumpmasters. Of this group there were three former Rangers: Corporal George Tatarakis, listed as killed while missing in action, Corporal Orlando W. Chada and MSG. William Kent.

The other airborne unit, the 187 the Regimental Combat Team (Airborne), provided many replacements to the 8240th Army Unit, however the majority of these replacements were assigned throughout the UN Partisan Infantry Regiments located on the island bases north of the front lines. In regards to the presence of the Ranger Companies and the 187th, one can only question why these units, earlier in the quest for qualified airborne, combat experienced personnel, were not pursued more aggressively for input to the unconventional warfare effort, especially the clandestine airborne effort. Captain Robert I. Channon of the 3d Airborne Infantry Ranger Company was placed on temporary duty with the Eighth Army Miscellaneous Group to assist in the evaluation and analysis of the Partisan bases on the West coast of Korea. He did an outstanding job and was subsequently reassigned to the 187th Regimental Combat Team. It is interesting to note that according to William B. Breuer, in his book, SHADOW WARRIORS, he cites the situation that occurred later in 1951 with the deactivation of the Rangers. Major General (then Major) Jack Singlaub approached the commander of the 187th to have Captain Channon transferred to Singlaub's CIA operation. The Commander, BG Trapnell, flatly refused to release Channon. It may be assumed that General Singlaub still had knowledge of the Rangers he had trained earlier at Fort Benning and now needed them.[8]

An unfortunate aspect of having been assigned to this unconventional warfare unit, regardless of the actual individual assignment, was the highly classified nature of the activity. This has caused many veterans that I have interviewed, to point out that their personnel records are incomplete, which means there is no mention of their actual duties and in one case the discharge papers do not even reflect service in Korea. It is not unusual to encounter some of these types of administrative problems, but in the case of the Korean initiative, the problems seem unusually high in numbers. As late as the 1990's many of the veterans were not aware of declassifications that had occurred, therefore they would not discuss their Korean wartime assignments.[9]

Regardless of the source of personnel assignments to the AVIARY operation, the qualifications for duty as a jumpmaster in this particular type of activity exceeds that of a jumpmaster assigned to a normal airborne unit. The normal unit planning cycle would have a joint meeting between jumpmasters, the airforce operations personnel, and the pilot and navigator. With larger formations the actual signal to jump may come from the lead aircraft rather than the jumpmaster making the decision, other than to observe the area for enemy ground fire or other obstacles that would cause concern for the drop.

The AVIARY jumpmasters were concerned with coordinated planning with the pilot and navigator to navigate to a pinpoint location, and with the verification of the drop zone. Additionally, the jumpmaster confronted with very small drop zones, often located in surrounding mountainous terrain must also coordinate speed and altitude of the aircraft in order to hit the drop zone. The pilot is concerned with the terrain he is flying over and the manner of approach to the drop zone that permits a low and slow drop mode. The aircraft must be able to clear the vertical obstacles near or immediately around the drop zone. Such skill, steady nerves and control of the indigenous personnel in the aircraft were absolutely necessary to execute such operations. Detailed later are parameters of drop zone strategy employed by me. Each jumpmaster of the AVIARY team was orientated on this strategy. The ultimate goal was to deliver the indigenous personnel as safely as possible on their exact drop zone. To do less was not acceptable and did lead to a few transfers out of AVIARY.

Prior to my assignment to the AVIARY team, I had experienced a combat jump in Europe during W.W.II, had completed 110 jumps between October 1942-January 1952, and was a graduate of the 82d Airborne Division Pathfinder and Jumpmaster Courses. During 1943 while with the 551st Parachute Infantry Battalion in Panama, I made many jumps on small drop zones in jungle areas of Panama. These jumps were usually company size or less so that experience was similar to many of the AVIARY missions flown.

My assistant, 2nd Lt. Albritton, and I possessed the same qualifications and interestingly enough, had served with me in the 551st during W.W.II. Emory Albritton, already a seasoned combat experienced paratrooper, had been wounded in the chest in Southern France during that campaign, wounded the second time by a gunshot to the stomach in the Battle of the Bulge. He even went AWOL from the hospital in France, returned to join the 509th Parachute Infantry Battalion where he fought at Born and St. Vith before the 509th was also deactivated. Emory finished the war with the 505th Parachute Infantry Regiment. I had no doubts about Emory's bravery and determination to complete in the best manner possible any task assigned to him. AVIARY missions were divided between the two officers, while the enlisted jumpmasters were rotated between the two officers. In many instances there were multiple missions on the same night so the enlisted jumpmasters would take their own mission. The philosophy in assigning missions was based upon the perceived, potential risk. The officers took the mission with the most risk; enlisted jumpmasters also went on these missions with the officers where additional jumpmasters were needed. In many instances the potential risk of loss was at the same level.

The reality is that two of the perceived less risky missions ended in tragedy for the enlisted jumpmasters. The first to be described later saw the C-46 aircraft sabotaged by an agent on board causing it to crash. Master Sgt. Harrison, the jumpmaster survived and became a POW, while the other two from the 8240th Army Unit were lost. The second mission lead by an enlisted jumpmaster Cpl. Robert F. Carver, (Jr.), was severely wounded by anti-aircraft fire while flying in a B-26 aircraft on a short penetration mission north of the bombline. Fortunately, Carver was not killed, but his wounds caused complete disability.

16

During the SPITFIRE operations British personnel participated in the operations, namely, Captain Ellery Anderson and Lt. Adams-Acton. Captain Anderson was injured on the initial drop but was evacuated and survived. Lt. Adams-Acton became a prisoner of war on a subsequent behind the lines operation and died while a prisoner of war.

As a general rule, the indigenous personnel that became either BAKER SECTION or AVIARY participants came into the program from various sources. Some were recruited from the North Korean refugees who fled south; others were part of the insurgency already participating in guerrilla warfare against the North Korean Army or Interior Security Forces. In addition to these, Korean civilians were recruited locally and given an alternative to service in the South Korean Army or to volunteer for service with the Partisan forces.

Another sources of recruits were both captured North Korean and Chinese volunteers who had been anti-Communists. Current knowledge of their former units, at time of capture, became invaluable in developing a cover story for operations as well as their documents that were readily usable and could also be copied to forge additional credentials for other agents. Under personal histories later in this book are details from one of the Chinese volunteers describing his activities with the 8240th Army Unit.

The perpetual problem faced by the US personnel was the language barrier[10]. The effort depended greatly on the Korean interpreters and in fact quite often for whatever purpose, the true meaning of English was not transmitted to the indigenous agents or partisans. This did cause some apprehension among the US personnel and not doubt caused a less than effective operation. In the case of Operation VIRGINIA I while evading enemy ground forces, a group of Korean partisans became separated from their US leaders, but turned-up later by exfiltrating the frontlines. Two of these partisans were later executed by the South Korean Army when it was discovered they had been captured by the North Korean Forces and sent south to be double agents[11]. One can readily recognize the difficulties within the clandestine airborne effort where last minute critical instructions had to be passed on to the agents on board, with the jumpmaster never knowing for sure that his instructions were correctly translated.

In late 1952, the US Army offered for assignment to the 8240th Army Unit, graduates of the newly established Special Forces classes at Fort Bragg, N. C. However, again even though these were well trained and airborne qualified, the language problem still existed. The language problem plagued the US Military through the end of the hostilities. With the failures of both VIRGINIA I and SPITFIRE, the use of US personnel on such missions was restricted. Caucasians with no language capability could not survive in that different cultural environment, especially without the ability to communicate with the local villagers. As recorded in the analysis of clandestine airborne operations both Generals Ridgway and General Collins, US Army Chief of Staff came to the same conclusion with the deactivation of the Ranger Infantry Companies (Airborne).

After the Special Forces school graduates joined the 8240th Army Unit, the Far East Command in reports to the Army Staff complained that the Special Forces program did not include language training. Subsequently, language training became an integral part of such training. The Lodge Act also facilitated enhancement of linguistically qualified personnel by authorizing the enlistment of alien personnel into the US Army. Many of these enlistees joined Special Forces, thereby, adding an element to the Special Forces capability to communicate with potential partisan forces in their native language. In 1956

I had a first hand opportunity to debrief many Hungarian Freedom fighters who crossed into Austria as the Soviet Forces put down the Hungarian uprising. Many of these freedom fighters enlisted in the US Army under the provisions of the Lodge Act.

The recent example of the Special Forces deployed to Afghanistan demonstrates the enhancement of the Special Operations Forces that now have worldwide language capabilities and, therefore, greater operations capabilities and control. Reliance upon interpreters by our SOF in operational areas has been greatly reduced.

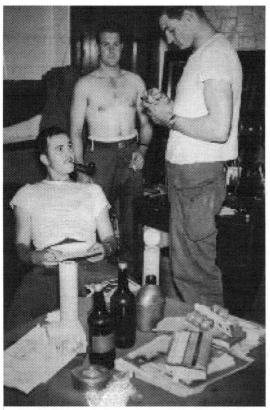

SGT Mast, CPL Carver, SGT Ramano, AVIARY Jumpmasters, relaxing in their quarters, Seoul, Korea.

AVIARY personnel in quarters, Seoul, Korea. LT Dillard, SGT Herbert, SGT Romano and MSG Kent - Jumpmasters.

Partisans ready to jump into North Korea; seen with LT Dillard - AVIARY, at Safehouse Jump School, Jul 52.

LT Keller and MAJ Dye, CO, Leopard Base, Paengyang-do with partisans, selected for AVIARY parachute training.

MAJ Austin, S2, CCRAK jumping on the Han River sandbar, Seoul, Korea. Jumpmaster - LT Dillard.

LT Dillard, AVIARY, on the beach at Yo Do, North Korea after making an air delivery of supplies to Partisans.

AVIARY, Korean Instructor,
Hong Youg.

Hong recovering his parachute after jumping with LT Dillard, Mar 52.

Korean Partisan stands in the door
for a training jump. SGT Vic Ramano
is the Jumpmaster, Mar 52.

Mr. Pak with Author, LT Dillard on Safehouse Training
Facility for AVIARY personnel.

Author, LT Dillard and Assistant,
LT Emory Albritton on AVIARY
mission over North Korean Mar 52.

Author, LT Dillard in C-46 on AVIARY mission
in early hours over North Korea, Feb 52.

Korean interpreters/instructors on the Han River sandbar drop zone after an AVIARY training jump, Mar 52.

Korean Partisans loading on a C-46, for training jump on the Han River sandbar, Mar 52.

Leopard Base Partisans landing on the Han River sandbar drop zone, Mar 52.

Leopard Base Partisans loading on trucks after jump on Paengyang-do, their home base.

Leopard Battalion Partisans after training jump on Han River sandbar drop zone, Mar 52.

Korean female Airborne Partisan aboard aircraft.

CHAPTER IV

LOGISTICS

As the clandestine airborne effort begin to expand, it became necessary to setup a dependable logistics support mechanism that would sustain the AVIARY element with airborne quartermaster items of equipment and materials. In early 1952 the AVIARY operational element was located in a large building in Seoul proper near the Headquarters, 8240th Army Unit. The AVIARY element was closed off from the rest of the headquarters. The space provided a small office or briefing room where a map of Korea was displayed, and files for aerial photographs and a large room for storage of personnel and cargo parachutes, aerial delivery containers and miscellaneous materials needed to rig the aerial delivery containers for airdrops.[1]

Adjacent to the storage was an exterior space with adequate height to permit the hanging of personnel parachutes for either drying or shaking out ground debris that had become entangled with the parachute when landing. These parachutes were those used by the AVIARY jumpmasters and the training jumps made by indigenous personnel. The parachutes both personnel and cargo were returned to the Quartermaster Depot at Brady Airfield in Japan for necessary repairs and repacking. Normally, a trip was scheduled monthly to make a direct exchange of parachutes and draw additional parachutes for forthcoming operations. The same applied to aerial delivery containers. In 1951, the Assistant Chief of Staff for Intelligence, Far East Command issued a classified letter referred to as "LS 51". It stated the bearer of the letter was to be accorded, on a priority basis, any request for support without question. However, any questions arising over its use may be reported to the Far East Command. This simple authority facilitated as well as eased procurement of any operational items.[2]

Obviously, the disposal of hundreds of personnel and cargo parachutes and aerial delivery containers raised questions, but the LS-51 muted them. The airdrops in North Korea resulted in the loss of this gear but did not require any accountability within the US Army supply system. Of course, the 8240th Army Unit Commander was ultimately responsible for the proper use of any US Army funds, supplies and material and was audited by the Inspector General of the Assistant Chief of Staff, Intelligence, Far East Command[3]

The periodic visits to the Quartermaster Depot in Japan also provided the AVIARY representatives a review of the airborne quartermaster stockage and to identify additional items needed in operations. On one such visit, the sections of aluminum rollers used to facilitate movement along the floor of the aircraft of aerial delivery containers was located and immediately requested. In addition, small, oval shaped waterproof containers were found in the warehouse that proved to be suitable in packing radio gear, some foodstuffs and ammunition. These containers made of a heavy gauge paper and waterproofed provided excellent storage containers for the agents and partisans to cache their operational materials for extended periods of time and protection from the elements.

In addition to my personal visits to the Depot, a point of contact was established with the Quartermaster personnel at the Depot whereby a call or message for a priority item would be handled immediately and shipped on the next available aircraft. Such contacts although very supportive did raise questions about the classified activity that required the AVIARY personnel to be very firm in not discussing its activities

With the logistics channel established for the airborne items to conduct operations, the AVIARY staff was able to be more selective in the type of aerial delivery container to use. It also had access to varying sizes of cargo chutes and the means via the aluminum roller delivery system to move cargo faster out of the plane, thereby improving pinpoint accuracy on the small drop zones.

Initially, small. colored lights on the aerial delivery containers had not been used. Often when the cargo drop was off the drop zone the indigenous personnel on the ground had difficulty in locating them. An assortment of lights and strips of spaghetti (luminous material) was also requisitioned and on a selective basis used on the operations. The choice depended upon the drop zone location, proximity to enemy or security forces, and the considered necessity to attach them to the aerial delivery containers.

In the past, in a crunch situation, without the logistic support, the clandestine airborne effort resorted to the use of barracks bags, ponchos, and heavily secured rope bundles that were then secured to either cargo or personnel parachutes or whatever was available and airdropped.

The establishment of this logistic backup to support the clandestine airborne effort proved invaluable. Operations could be better planned and the actual airdrop more efficiently handled simply because the material needed to properly execute these missions was finally available to AVIARY on a continuous basis. In spite of the classified nature of the AVIARY operation more cooperation on the part of the Quartermaster depot staff could not have been more supportive.[4]

Aerial delivery containers and associated parachutes used in Korea

**A5 container dropped
with a G1A parachute**

**A6 container mounted
on a light aircraft**

A7 container with a G1A parachute

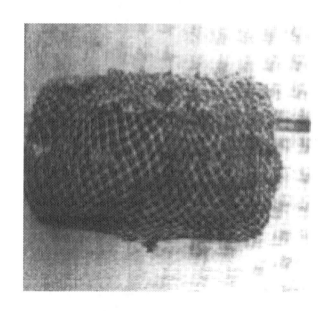

A10 delivery container

**A5 and A22 container with a G1A
parachute delivering field rations**

Aerial delivery container used in Korea

**Aerial delivery using a
personnel reserve parachute**

**Rope type aerial delivery of
field rations**

**Rigging oil drums for aerial
delivery with an A22 container**

**Rope aerial delivery container
to parachute drop field rations**

**Barb wire rigged for aerial delivery using
*aircraft rollers***

**Concertina wire rigged for aerial delivery using
*aircraft rollers***

CHAPTER V

THE COURAGEOUS COURIER

I have chosen the title of Chapter V, in recognition and respect for Lieutenant Colonel Jerome J. Pratt, US Army- Retired. Pratt is the US Army authority on the History of United States Army Pigeon Service. Pratt served in the Army Pigeon Service for most of his active duty experience. Except for the descriptions of missions of homing pigeons during the Korean War by elements of the 8240th Army Unit, most of the following information is taken from Pratts' Book, COURAGEOUS COURIERS. MEMOIRS OF A PIGEON SOLDIER, published by American Pigeon Journal Co., Warrenton, Missouri, 63383, May 1977.

With the advances in communications developed during World War II, it was inconceivable that the U S Army would still be in the Pigeon Service in the 1950's. However the US Army Signal Corps maintained Pigeon Service Units until 1957. The last unit was deactivated, the active duty personnel reassigned throughout the Army and the remaining 1,018 homing pigeons sold to the public. LTC. Pratt has recorded in his book, that a requirement for Korea was developed "for speedy, yet mobile, means of communications to serve small probing patrols". It is assumed this was the classified version for the requirement meant to serve the agents and partisans operating behind the lines.

In July 1951, according to Pratt, 60 homing pigeons were shipped to Korea. The handling of the birds required skill and patience. An experimental loft was mounted on a one-ton trailer, similar to that used successfully in Europe during W.W.II. The principal element that utilized these homing pigeons was the 1st US Corps. Its location near Seoul facilitated fast recovery and delivery of the messages the homing pigeons brought to the Pigeon Loft and further transport to the 8240th Army Unit. Pratt's opinion that the inexperience of the I Corps Pigeoneers resulted in achieving only a 57 mile distance for these birds to home- in on the newly located pigeon loft, during the initial seven week period in Korea.

The additional problem encountered was high numbers of losses as these pigeons fell prey to Korean hawks. Reports indicated that a total of 116 pigeons were sent to Korea, where 20 became food for the hawks. These losses influenced the Signal Corps to dismantle the operation and ship the remaining pigeons to Fort Monmouth, NJ, where they arrived September 12, 1954. LTC Pratt feels that a dozen of his experienced pigeoneers of his day would have overcome the Korean problems and been more successful. The Korean requirement called for homing distances up to 200 miles. Success was obtained and the homing pigeons ranged as far as the banks of the Yalu.[1]

No doubt these US Army pigeons were employed by the agents and partisans of the 8240th Army Unit, as well as augmented by pigeons that were procured and trained in Japan. The need for an additional means of communications with the agents and partisan units that were deployed behind the lines, influenced the deployment of the US Army Pigeon Service to Korea. It provided additional means of communicating, at a critical time in the operations, facilitated verification of successful clandestine airborne operations as well establishing the location of the operational base.[2]

21

Well into 1951, many of the clandestine airborne operations were written off as a failure since, after the drop, no further communications were received from the agents or partisans. Therefore, the operational headquarters did not know if the drops were successful. In an attempt to track the clandestine airborne drops, the use of homing pigeons were employed for use in two ways.

Upon landing the agent or partisan leader would prepare a short message indicating the landing was a success and the equipment had been recovered. The first homing pigeon was equipped with a capsule on its leg in which the message was placed and the pigeon then released just before daylight. The pigeons would not fly during darkness. The second pigeon would be handled in the same manner, but after the personnel had reached their operational base and checked their equipment. This required that the second pigeon be held for another day if the move to the operational base was a lengthy march and the pigeon was not released late in the evening of the first day.

I have rigged many of the indigenous agents and partisans with homing pigeons and many messages were successfully received by the 8240th Army Unit. Although most messages were prepared, as the agent had been instructed to do it, one message came in with both good and bad news. It read 'As I sit on this hill and see the beautiful sunrise, I think of my country and what I can do for it". The good news is that the airborne drop had been a success. Subsequently, the agent's radio message did come on the air and the operation proceeded as planned. The other warning to the agent or partisan was that the homing pigeon was an important part of the operation and was NOT A MEAL![3]

Not widely known, but accounted for in Pratt's book is the fact that on D-Day 80 of 600 civilian loaned pigeons were strapped to the chests of US Paratroopers that jumped in France on June 6, 1944. However, only four came home of the 80 birds from England, none carried messages, but three of the four were covered with blood, presumably from their paratrooper carriers. There were four other pigeons from Plymouth, England that did return with messages from the Normandy beaches that day.[4]

In the case of the Korean agents and partisans as the personnel were rigged for their parachute jump, the homing pigeons were delivered by the team leaders to AVIARY. The AVIARY jumpmaster would place the reinforced cardboard container on the breast of the jumper and secure the cage to the parachute harness. The cages, themselves contained two separated compartments in which a homing pigeon would be placed in each side. The homing pigeon already had a capsule attached to its leg, so the indigenous personnel had only to insert the message into the capsule and release the pigeon.

The jumper was instructed to not handle the pigeon or give the pigeon any food or water. There is always danger in damaging the bird or otherwise influencing the bird to become disoriented. The jumpers were impressed with the knowledge that if their bird is released in the darkness, it will wait in the area for daylight and may become a victim of foul play. If released at the beginning of early morning nautical twilight (BEMNT), the bird will begin its flight home immediately.[5]

It was well known among the communications personnel at the 8240th headquarters and the AVIARY staff that one bird in particular had been used on several missions, had one leg severed, presumably from small arms fire, but still survived. Recognition was made on two occasions for example, "GI JOE", who was awarded the Dicken Medal for gallantry in W.W.II for being credited with saving the lives of many British soldiers in the capture of the Italian village, Colvi Vecchia, October 18, 1943. On display in the

National Museum of American History's Armed Forces Hall, is Cher Ami, the stuffed homing pigeon of W.W.I. Cher Ami made many missions for the US Army and was finally mortally wounded. The French Government awarded a medal to Cher Ami for his bravery. The Korean birds, as courageous as they were on their missions, are not even a footnote in military history.[6]

In researching the unclassified records of the US Army Signal Corps, and in discussions with the US Army Historian at Fort Gordon, Georgia there is no record of the employment of the US Army Pigeon Service in Korea. However, the unclassified records show homing pigeons of the Signal Corps were shipped to Korea. Fortunately, after fifty years since the end of hostilities in Korea, the use of homing pigeons as late as the 1950s is still significant in the military history of their usage and should be recorded. It is believed that the 8240th Army Unit was the last US Army unit to employ homing pigeons in combat operations.

In the present state of advanced technological communications, it is still surprising to learn that in the Police Department of Orissa, India there are currently 27 police pigeon cages (lofts) and it is the duty of 37 policemen to feed and train the birds. Such pigeon message service dates back to 1946, about the time of India's independence from Great Britain was granted and the birds turned over to the police. Training starts at about six week of age, with gradual training extending the homing distance up to 310 miles. After having a meal of wheat and millet, they return home. In 1999, these homing pigeons were used after a cyclone tore into the region, killing 8495 people and destroying communications throughout the region. The homing pigeons saved the day in reestablishing communications links with the coastal areas[7]. Today, in France, homing pigeons are used by medical facilities to ferry blood samples from small medical facilities to larger testing centers.[8]

As I researched this subject I became more interested and felt that this chapter should provide more background and history of the "Heroic Birds." The Sultan of Baghdad used these Heroic Birds to support military operations as early as 1150. They were also used as postal messengers for over 800 years. The records of the French Revolution of 1848 reveal these messengers were utilized to carry messages from Paris to French and Belgian newspapers beyond the battle field as well as to carry messages over areas that were not serviced by the early telegraph lines of that time.

The development of pigeon racing is traceable to the Belgians in 1818 when they staged 100-mile races. This sport was taken up by the French and British who developed their own pigeon clubs. The Roman Legions utilized pigeons as messengers to keep the Roman public informed on day to day status of its campaigns. It appears that the Romans were the innovators of the courier service using homing pigeons as a part of their regular communications. According to a description in the book, Heroic Birds, by Arch Whitehouse, the noted Roman politician, Marcus Junius Brutus, utilized many domesticated pigeons as messengers to transmit and receive important tactical information that greatly aided in breaking Marc Anthony's siege of Modena.

Although not related directly to transmitting military tactical information the use of pigeons as messengers during the battle for Waterloo in Belgium and its outcome had a tremendous commercial influence for the Rothschild brothers. The outcome of the Battle of Waterloo had potential for fortunes in the world stock markets depending upon who the victor would be. The Rothschild's set up their financial network throughout the key cities of Europe and in so doing established a private news service that included the utilization of homing pigeons. This facet of their communications system was to bear fruit in a very simple way.

While the Battle of Waterloo raged for days, the world markets waited anxiously for the outcome that would effect the fortunes of many. Should the British win, French stock values would diminish, including its exchange values. Should the French win similarly the British stock and exchange values would plummet. The critical importance of information, either military or commercial, as in this instance, cannot be understated. For about 30 hours the battle raged, while the commercial world held its breath. A Rothschild agent named Rothworth carrying a still ink smudged Dutch newspaper, traveled from Ostend, Belgium and met Nathan Rothschild at Folkstone Harbor, England. This was the 19th of June. Rothschild read the news then returned to London.

Upon his arrival in London, Rothschild immediately sold all their holdings of British consols. This move on his part influenced the public to unload their holdings, thereby driving down to value of the British securities. Once the values hit rock bottom, Rothschild bough a tremendous amount at these bottom level prices. Very shortly after the news of the British victory became known, the values of the British securities soared to new heights. Apparently, this transaction, based on advanced information, was the single most important financial deal of the Rothschilds. This story is legend but possibly no entirely true.

During World War I, pigeons were used in ever expanding numbers. Agents operating inside enemy territory were provided pigeons by either balloon landing or drops by parachute. In some instances German defectors used pigeons to indicate their placement and access to conduct espionage or to deliver classified documents in their possession. One such agent was recruited via this means when a pigeon he released was intercepted by the British. Contact was made and the agent turned over documents to the British that covered a great majority of German order of battle as well as information about the unit commanders of these German units.

One operation that is analogous to the Airborne clandestine operations of the Korean War reminds one that in love and war there are few new developments. For example, in March 1918, the German General Staff, desperate for a victory planned the operation with great hopes of success. The Allied High Command had detected some indication of a large scale attack by the Germans, but did not know from where the major effort would begin. They realized the railroad and roadways in the German held areas provided relatively good access routes for their reserves. The German reserves had been strategically located so as to facilitate a rapid move of these forces to reinforce their main attacking forces.

While Allied intelligence had good coverage of the enemy forces and rear areas, their great shortfall in intelligence coverage was the Grand Duchy of Luxembourg. The agent needed for this mission had to assimilate himself into the local populace in order to survive and move around on his collection mission. This situation is similar to the problems the UN Forces were confronted with in Korea. The presence of non-Asian qualified personnel truly inhibited the Korean collection mission. In this instance the agent needed for the mission must be from the area. The Luxemburgers, Teutonic in origin, but generally sympathetic to the Allied cause, still presented a problem in finding the right person to become an espionage agent in Luxembourg.

Fortunately, British intelligence located a Major Steffen, a Major in the British Army who also happened to be a native Luxemburger. The Major, eager to participate in combat operations readily accepted the task. The mission was to drop the agent by parachute into Luxembourg. The parachute was the type that had been used by the Kite-Balloon observers. For communications the agent would carry along a basket of pigeons to be used for the transmission of messages. The pilot of the aircraft had flown many bombing missions over Luxembourg so the pilot was felt to be well qualified to locate the drop zone without difficulty. The distance to the drop zone was about 150 miles and after about 90 minutes of flying the agent jumped with the pigeons. The landing was very successful, as it was on target with no problems encountered.

Major Steffen recovered his gear and walked cross-country to his home, a farm near Ettelbruck. He made contact with his family and with their assistance successfully conducted his collection and reporting until the end of the war. Most of his reporting was about the presence and status of the German reserves in Luxembourg but it aided the Allied High Command in anticipating moves by the German General Staff. As I researched this story I compared the similar problems experienced in Korea, trying to conduct operations successfully with limitations due to language, and cultural and physical appearance of Caucasian operatives in an Asian society.

My research also provided answers to several questions that naturally arise about the training and utilization of these heroic birds. For example, birds are trained over a period of time in order to expand their range of operations. Training of these birds, "Squeakers" as they are called, begins with them being placed on the tops of the pigeon lofts to become visually familiar with the surrounding countryside. When they are eight weeks old they begin flying for one hour intervals twice a day, flying in wide circles around their lofts. After this initial period of flying around the local area they are placed in baskets and given rough rides over the country side to adjust to the bumps and grinds they will be exposed to when they become operational. These expanded ranges of up to five miles then begin to identify those birds who do not measure up to the rigorous routine the birds will be constantly exposed to when they are operational. Birds have a natural aversion to flying over water, including rivers and streams. Additional training is needed to overcome the fear of flying over bodies of water. Their proclivity to fly around such bodies of water had to be negated in order to conserve their energy and strength for long range flights.

Birds also are subject to weather conditions. Inclement weather influenced the birds to fly low just above the terrain features that also make them good targets for enemy marksmen, however, during good weather the birds fly at very high altitudes. Those birds that have succeeded in completing the initial training then begin advanced military training by being released 125 miles from their lofts. The birds' ranges are continually increased. During this phase of training many of the birds do fail to return to their lofts.

Training continues for about seven months. Those birds still in the program then start a more advanced training program such as releases from varying distances, in opposite directions and their ability to locate and identify their own loft. One of the most difficult tests for the birds is to be released from either an aircraft or surface naval vessel about fifty miles off-shore. The birds must initially locate land then fly to its loft as quickly as possible. Birds do not like to fly in darkness, usually they will land at night await the morning light then fly to their loft. Consideration of these factors must be planned in the briefing of the personnel who will release the birds. If the range is very long and the release is in the late evening, it is possible when darkness descends, the bird will land and roost for the night, then fly out the following morning, thereby, delaying the delivery of the very important message.

During World War II most naval vessels and many aircraft carried pigeon sets for emergency purposes. The crews were briefed to avoid getting the birds wet. When the feathers become wet the birds lose their lift capability, thereby, reducing the bird's ability to rise to any height or move forward. Pigeons were also trained to do a "dead drop", that is the bird had to learn to keep its wings folded until clear of the slip stream of the aircraft since failure to do so caused a brief period of disorientation that delayed their reorientation to the right direction toward their home base.

During the operation where thousand of British troops had withdrawn to the beaches at Dunkirk, hundreds of these birds were release by the British troops. They carried to England messages for help in evacuating the troops from Dunkirk. Thousands of British civilians in all type of boats sailed to the rescue. About 330.000 troops were evacuated by this means due largely to the messages the pigeons carried home. Apparently the last pigeon to be released contained the famous message of General Lord Gort, "All clear". Not to be overlooked, the same situation occurred at Dieppe in 1942, when the Canadian Commandos landed at Dieppe and ran into deadly German defense forces. Again, the resort to carrier pigeons facilitated radio silence and also advised the Command of the need to begin a withdrawal of the Canadian Commandos.

American trainers developed carrier pigeon operations at Fort Monmouth, Fort Benning and Fort Sam Houston. The trainers at Fort Monmouth concentrated on training the birds to fly at night. By increasingly exposing the birds to short range night flying, they gradually overcame the birds' proclivity to resist night flying. Additionally, the trainers worked many long hours to develop a bird that could make a two-way trip, for example from division to corp and return. The system was eventually developed when it was recognized by the trainers that upon the birds' arrival at the home loft they were fed without water, upon release they headed for the field loft and water was provided.

The heroic birds fell prey to all types of nature and manmade devices. With the presence of hawks the Germans employed during World War I, the birds were quite often attacked and destroyed. The French developed a device to defend the birds. It was an old Chinese device whereby bamboo whistles were placed on the birds' tail feathers. The birds' slipstream provided sufficient wind to blow the whistles thereby frightening away the hawks. These antihawk whistles were still used by the United States Army Pigeon Service through the period of World War II.

Intelligence services also considered the potential for compromise of the information contained in the capsule on the bird's leg if it was injured or killed and fell into enemy hands. One procedure was to carefully wrap the message containing the classified information in a bird's feather and insert it under the birds' feathers, placing the decoy message in the capsule. If the bird fell into enemy hands the classified information may not be discovered. The reader may feel this lengthy dissertation on the history of the heroic birds is trivia, however, one must also consider the potential for a catastrophic conflict that would bomb us back to using bows and arrows and heroic birds!

CHAPTER VI

SELECTED CLANDESTINE AIRBORNE OPERATIONS

VIRGINIA I:

This part of the book is devoted to succinct descriptions of selected clandestine airborne operations that were conducted during the Korean War by either elements of Korean Liaison Office, the US Army Eighth Army Miscellaneous Group's 8086th Army Unit (BAKER SECTION) and the AVIARY TEAM of the 8240th Army Unit. It is necessary to identify these groups as reorganizations occurred and blurs the specifics of which unit should be credited for these wartime operations. The US personnel who conducted these operations are quite proud of their combat participation in classified activities, and their units. There is every intention, in this book, to recognize both.

The first recorded clandestine airborne mission of a partisan nature was conceptualized by Colonel McGee and his staff of the US Eighth Army, Miscellaneous Group to support Army planners in their attempts to shut down the east coast rail line. This line ran from Wonsan, along the east coast to Kosong, then inland through the Diamond Mountains. Colonel McGee's original plan was changed from a US Army Rangers operation to a US Ranger led group that included combat experienced Koreans. Additionally, the target was changed and now would be the railroad tunnel, southwest of Hyon-ni, North Korea. The team had only five weeks to train for the mission. The target was located about thirty miles inland from the Sea of Japan. Unlike other rail lines, this line was standard gauge, therefore, steam-powered engines could travel over these lines, coupled with the numerous rail line tunnels in this area, the sabotage of this line was an ideal mission[1]

With the target selected and a date scheduled, the next task was to identify and gather the saboteurs, needed to execute the VIRGINIA I operation. The Miscellaneous Group had neither qualified US or Korean airborne personnel nor experienced demolitionists needed for the task. The staff of BAKER SECTION did offer a limited number of airborne qualified personnel, however, these personnel were needed to continue training and other operations and the problem of qualified demolitionists still needed to be addressed.

With regards to Korean personnel, two groups of twenty Korean OCS candidates were made available as volunteers who would receive their commissions without attending the OCS course. The plan called for each group to cross train to become airborne qualified and also to become demolitionists. However, not all went well, of the forty volunteers, only two remained in the program and participated in another mission. During the airborne training jump phase, the pilot missed the drop zone, which resulted in eleven men suffering fractured bones while another nine were badly bruised. This occurred due to misjudged wind speed and the jumpers' parachute landing falls made on several frozen rice paddies where the strong, gusty ground winds blew the jumpers along the frozen ground.

These unfortunate happenings during the initial training forced a change in the plans.

The schedule was changed so the personnel would receive four weeks of demolition and other sabotage related training and only one day of parachute qualification with no practice jumps. The actual combat jump would be their first jump on a nighttime operation in unfamiliar territory. This revised program having been decided by Colonel McGee, now needed US combat experienced, airborne qualified personnel.

Colonel McGee turned to the most readily available source of such men, The Ranger Infantry Companies (Airborne). Recall that earlier in the initiation of the partisan effort, Captain Robert I. Channon of the Third Ranger Infantry Company, (Airborne) was borrowed to assist in resolving partisan differences out on the island bases, so it was no surprise to seek help from the Rangers once again.

On February 15, 1951, the Fourth US Army Ranger Infantry Company (Airborne) provided four Ranger volunteers "wishing to participate in a mission behind enemy lines."[2] These four Rangers were interviewed by Colonel McGee and his staff and accepted for the operation. As alluded to earlier in this article, the four were enlisted men; three were corporals and one a private first class. The three corporals were combat experienced. Corporal Martin Watson was a W.W.II Ranger, captured at Mount Cassino, Italy. Corporal Edward Pucel had served in the OSS in Yugoslavia and Greece while Corporal Edward T. Miles' combat was in Korea. And private first class Baker was a former para-marine with combat time in the Pacific during W.W.II.

With this combination of experience such as Escape and Evasion by Pucel Miles' considerable demolitions training and experience, Baker's radio/communications, and Watson's several assault landings, the US team seemed well equipped for the mission.[3]

With the training proceeding and the Rangers now with the US Army Aerial Delivery Detachment, briefings proceeded with the use of aerial photographs, maps and a sand table that had been made of the target area. Remember this was to be a night jump on an unfamiliar dropzone. Already rejected was the Rangers' request that a pathfinder team be dropped to locate and mark the drop zone for the subsequent landing of the main body. The Rangers did not have much opportunity to get to know the Koreans who would accompany them on the mission. The Rangers finally met them on the day the Koreans were to receive their jump training. As Evanhoe points out in his book," the Rangers had only 52 hours before the jump to work with their counterparts".[4]

The mission was planned to be completed in seventy-two hours from the landing until the water exfiltration off the coast, which was thirty miles away. The scheduling of this operation in March was bad timing due to the freezing temperatures and the constant strong winds that made it exceedingly difficult to move cross country as they must do to exfiltrate. However, the mission was set to go anyway.

A C-47 aircraft was selected for the mission. Although not known for certain, one could surmise the C-47 could fly low and slow for the drop to better insure hitting the unmarked drop zone. The other alternative would have been the use of a C-46, since the team and equipment was too great for the B-26. The approximate three-hour flight from K-3 departed at 2000 hours March 15. Extra flight time was necessary for the aircraft to fly a circuitous route, not directly to the target area. The target was about 250 miles from the Pusan area and at an altitude of 3000 feet. Weather conditions there did not favor the ground effort, especially when the exfiltration of the team had to be executed.[5]

As alluded to in the earlier description of dressing properly for these missions, the VIRGINIA I team experienced extreme cold due to the icy wind from the open jump

28

door, and the length of exposure to freezing temperature in the aircraft. Together with the airsickness suffered by the Korcans did not bode well for the operation.

This was an operational night jump similar to the earlier training jump in Pusan that had been such a failure. The Korean volunteers had been dropped off the drop zone as the winds were miscalculated, so was this operational night jump. A mountain meadow was incorrectly identified as the drop zone that was actually several miles south of Hyonni. The jumpers were scattered about over a wide area, about 8 miles away from the target drop zone. The wide dispersion pattern saw Miles and one Korean group land on the mountain slopes above where Pucel landed with his group in a valley. Baker and five Koreans landed on the far side of the mountain. Watson with four Koreans landed in the middle of the village of Ulchon-ni, actually between the village and Miles location. The village was about 9 miles south of Hynon-ni. The village's barking dogs woke the villagers who no doubt saw the Miles' party recovering their parachutes and moving through the village.[6]

In spite of the miserable drop, no one was injured, the equipment was recovered, and. presumably, the group leaders determined they missed the drop zone but felt they landed below it and therefore, all groups headed for the mountain rally point from different directions. Baker and Watson's groups met as they climbed the slope. Meanwhile, the weather became a storm with gale force winds and the deep snow made progress very difficult reducing visibility and making map reading almost impossible. The mission control aircraft did overfly the area each night, but the teams were unable to make contact because their radio batteries froze and the faint glow of their flashlights could not be observed at any distance[7]

The groups had jumped in the early morning hours of March 15th, however due to missing the dropzone and the awful weather conditions; they did not reach the rally point until the daylight of March 18. Efforts were made to signal the mission control aircraft by laying out panels however the greatly reduced visibility made the panels undetectable and could not be observed from above. Finally there was a break in the weather, but crews in friendly aircraft flying in the area never saw the panels.

The groups moved to the ridge above Hyon-ni and sent down a reconnaissance element dressed in NKPA uniforms. After observing the heavily defended positions at the tunnel entrances this target was then aborted and the groups moved back to the rally point. Once again, the groups heard the mission control aircraft circle their area but no contact was made with it. Finally by March 21st, it would appear the Headquarters wrote off the VIRGINIA I OPERATION.[8]

Corporal Watson, who had assumed command of the group decided to head toward the coast for the awaiting exfiltration boat and should it appear possible an attempt would be made to sabotage the rail line tunnel near Samdae-ri on the way to the coast. However, the sabotage mission was not to be. It was determined that this tunnel was also used as an air raid shelter and was heavily guarded. The groups buried their equipment, demolitions, prepared booby-traps, and also set a timed fuse to explode in forty-eight hours. The groups carried their radios and batteries in hope the batteries would regain strength in the sunlight. They would need the radios to contact the ship that was to await their exfiltration. As luck would have it, Miles tried a radio and it suddenly began to operate. This was now the 29th of March, considerably more time than the 72 hours that had been schedule for mission completion. Miles made contact with a 7th Division

Forward Air Controller (FAC) who immediately recognized him as VIRGINIA I. All front-line units had been alerted to be on the watch for these personnel who would exfiltrate through their lines. It required an extended voice communication to provide the necessary coded location of the group and its condition.[9]

About fours hours after the contact with the FAC, a BAKER SECTION mission controller, Captain Perry, arrived over the area in a C-47 and began communicating with Miles. The mission controller arranged for a return night resupply drop for that evening. With all this activity, including the presence of the troop carrier aircraft circling over the area, the enemy was alerted and began moving into the area. An alternative plan, code name DALLAS, had been arranged as a potential means of rescuing the men after they failed to report in after the drop on March 15.[10]

DALLAS planned for helicopters to rescue a maximum of 23 men who went on operation VIRGINIA I. Additionally, Lt. Wingate of the Miscellaneous Group staff was still aboard HMS Alacrity, awaiting signals to take a small boat ashore for the pickup. Three Sikorsky helicopters were made available for the rescue that would require three round trips to lift out all the men. At about 0800 hours, March 31st, the helicopters crossed the coast flying to the rendezvous point. In addition, a flight of Corsairs provided the air cover and close ground support against enemy ground forces. After gaining radio contact with VIRGINIA I, it was reported that the landing zone was under heavy enemy fire.[11]

At this point rather than abort, Lt. (jg) John H. Thornton, the senior pilot decided to attempt the first landing, however, his engine was hit by ground fire and he crashed near the landing zone (LZ). Although shaken up, but not injured, he with the help of Corporal Watson, under intense small arms fire made it to the LZ where the others were. The second helicopter came in and lifted out Miles and Pucel, however Miles was wounded in the face while being lifted. The third helicopter came in and begin lifting Baker when the winch became jammed. Due to this hitch and the strong winds, the pilot had no choice but to leave the area with the Ranger dangling beneath his helicopter. The pilot landed on a small nearby island so Baker could be release from the winch into the control of friendly partisans. The pilot then flew to the Coral Sea. In spite of an all out close air support by aircraft from the Coral Sea and HMS Black Swan. The LZ came under intense fire as infiltrating enemy forces closed in. Corporal Watson called in an air strike on the LZ, as they started working their way away from it.[12]

Watson and Lt. (jg) Thornton and five Koreans escaped the trap, but lost their radio. Now this group, on its own again, had no means to arrange for an alternate pickup. At some time during that night the Koreans became separated from the Americans. It cannot be confirmed, but it is possible, the Koreans felt they could survive by not being with the Americans, should they be observed during their movements cross country. Two of the Koreans that were on this operation survived and later came through the lines, but upon their interrogation, the South Korean Army interrogators learned the two had been captured and made double agents by the North Koreans. They were executed by the South Korean Army.[13]

For the two remaining Americans, they continued to make their way cross-country by hiding in mountain huts. Thornton developed serious foot problems as he was wearing flight boots that gave no protection against the ice, snow and freezing water. Finally, after a week of evading capture, Thornton could barely hobble so he decided to turn himself in to the police in Imbong-ni near Yangugu. His buddy, Watson, was captured when he ran into a North Korean Army patrol that had been searching the Yangugu area. At his time of capture, Watson was less than five miles from the frontlines. Both men were repatriated at the end of the War.[14]

The VIRGINIA I operation was a very ambitious plan with a constrained timetable to accomplish rather impossible tasks in the wintry mountainous terrain of North Korea. The absence of good intelligence regarding the tunnels' security would have negated this mission in the first instance. The mission was doomed almost from its beginning, and the airdrop was a total failure, even though the Rangers and their Korean counterparts were smart enough to find and regroup at the rally point. But their physical exhaustion in getting to the rally point in such awful subzero weather is strong testimony to the great leadership traits of the Rangers. One can only salute their skill, Yankee ingenuity and commitment to accomplish an impossible mission. They really tried!

SPITFIRE:

Operation SPITFIRE was developed with the idea of initiating the establishment of a partisan base in North Korea, with an American/British led force of Korean volunteers parachuting into the area and gathering disparate groups such as South Korean stragglers, anti-Communists and existing partisan elements that still survived in the area. After the withdrawal of United Nations forces, this cadre would become the operatives of the SPITFIRE base. This group would conduct intelligence collection, conduct attacks on the enemy infrastructure, perform sabotage; thereby, influencing the deployment of enemy combat forces away from the front. Eighth Army approved the plan. Personnel selection, organization of the force and other logistics to execute the operation began.

The tactical area of operations was to encompass about forty-eight hundred square miles, basically ringed by highways with referencing points such as Wonson on the east coast, Pyongyang on the northwest, again the second line, Wonson extending to Ch'orwon an eastern boundary. The southern boundary was linked between Ch'orwon to Sibyon-ni, while the western line extended between Sibyon-ni to Yul-li. This centralized placement of an operational base would facilitate extended operations over an area that contained main supply routes, railroad lines, as well as enemy troop movements and the local infrastructure.[1]

Sat'ae mountain provided an excellent potential for the operational base. During W.W. II, Japanese forces operated a logging camp in this area with prisoner of war labor. During this period the bubonic plaque killed many prisoners, guards and local civilians as it spread through this area. As a result, the local populace avoided venturing into this area fearing encounters with demons or ghosts. Also, this central plateau location would provide greater freedom of movement by the partisans without fear of locals observing their activity. This was especially important from an airborne planner's perspective. The airdrop resupply missions would be needed to support the effort. The planners were also glad to note the aerial reconnaissance of the area did not reveal any significant presence or activity by either the local populous or enemy forces.[2]

Next came the selection of the drop zone for the pathfinder team to use. As mentioned earlier in Chapter II, Strategy and Techniques, preparation proceeded in hand with the pilot and navigator to ensure total coordination of the effort. In regards to reconnaissance, unlike VIRGINIA I, aerial reconnaissance as well as a thorough map reconnaissance was done to ensure selection of the best possible drop zone, such as shortest route to it, avoidance of enemy antiaircraft gun positions, use of defilade of the hill and mountain mass to screen the drop, and most importantly, the use of distinctive landmarks, unlike others in the area that influenced easy identification of the drop zone. All these conditions were considered and woven into the framework for this mission. Finally, with the selection of a bowl shaped DZ that was five miles in length provided for a low approach for both personnel and resupply drops. The DZ, provided a softer landing for the jumpers since it was covered with small sized pines and thick growths of other plants, therefore the potential for jumper injuries was considerably less than VIRGINIA I. Additionally, the nearest town of significance was Karyoju-ri, located five miles southeast of the DZ.[3]

Another facet of this DZ location was its proximity to mountainous and wooded terrain that afforded many areas that could be utilized in evasion and escape measures if the SPITFIRE personnel were discovered by enemy forces. The intelligence collection effort could also take advantage of the terrain elevation to observe enemy activity, especially troop movements along the main supply routes that bound the operational area. Although, these factors favored the operation, it also offered a potential for compromise since the concept called for expanded and continual usage of the specific DZ area for the logistical support that had to be airdropped. Such continuous aerial activity, especially with troop carrier aircraft, would certainly not go unnoticed by air defense observers and/or radar station operators, as we shall see.[4]

With the coordination and final DZ selection we now turn to the operational expects of the airborne portions of the mission. As alluded too earlier in this book, a pathfinder team was not used in VIRGINIA I as had been considered and rejected by Colonel McGee. In this operation it was included and the operations planned for execution in four phases:

1st phase code name-THUNDER- would consist of a pathfinder team composed of Captain Ellery Anderson, British Army, and an experienced former member of the British SAS. Captain Anderson had joined BAKER SECTION prior to the VIRGINIA I mission and had run the Demolition-Sabotage School-preparing partisans for such missions. He would be accompanied by Sgt. William T. Miles, former Ranger and a veteran of the VIRGINIA I mission who was now assigned to BAKER SECTION from his old Fourth Ranger Company (Airborne). Additionally Sgt. Marvin G. Garner's communication skills were needed. Since he was a continuous wave (CW) operator, he carried an ANGRC-9 radio. The final complement included two Koreans and an English speaking interpreter, Song Chang Ok, and 3d Lt. Ho Yong Chong of the S. Korean Army. Ho had been one of the volunteer cadets for VIRGINIA I but did not participate in the mission.[5] A backup radio operator was also provided by British Fusilier George Mills, British Army who would jump with Anderson.

2nd phase LIGHTENING would be the first augmentation to the pathfinder team and contribute to the gradual buildup of the personnel strength. The team consisted of 1st Lt. David Hearn, the experienced veteran of airborne and guerrilla operations, as well as British Army 2d Lt. Leo Samuel Adams-Acton. He was fluent in Chinese as a result of being raised in Canton, China. Adams-Acton was also a graduate of Sandhurst. He had been recruited by Captain Anderson and really was neither airborne qualified nor had he any experience in these unconventional operations, however, Captain Anderson strongly supported his acceptance into BAKER SECTION. Also jumping were eleven Koreans assigned to the operation as part of the first augmentation to the mission.[6]

3d phase-STORM- consisted of the second personnel augmentation consisting of twenty additional Korean partisans. It was anticipated that this phase would have become rather routine and based on the two prior personnel jumps coupled with the successful resupply drops, the operation would soon be in full swing.[7]

4th phase-NORTHWIND- would see the remaining twenty Korean partisans completing the personnel augmentation that would then support the full range of combat operations planned for operation SPITFIRE. The basic plan hopefully would provide for the activation of three partisan operational bases from which operations against enemy forces would be conducted and expanded across central Korea extending from coast to coast. Captain Anderson in his book, BANNER OVER PUSAN, envisioned a greatly expanded effort that would sustain the operational bases but would still be totally dependent upon its personnel replacements and logistical support being provided by airborne delivery.[8]

As you will recall in reading about VIRGINIA I and the terrible communications problems experienced, in the planning for SPITFIRE, the operational teams were provided several of the US Army's newly developed infantry radios. The new PRC-10 was a frequency modulated (FM) radio. At that time the enemy forces could not monitor the FM bands so that security feature favored the operation. The radio was lighter than the old PRC-300, and the batteries for the PRC-10 lasted much longer. The pathfinder team leader, Anderson, and his assistant, Sgt. Miles, each carried a PRC-10, while Sgt. Garner carried the longer range, ANGRC-9 Continuous Wave (CW) set.[9] Lt. Adams-Acton would also bring along two PRC-10 radios and one ANGRC-9 CW set as part of his augmentation group. With this array of the new PRC-10 radios and the two ANGRC-9 CW sets, the operational base had backup radio communications for voice and/or the longer range CW sets. The planners felt this plan provided more than enough radio communications support. After the VIRGINIA I failures, the BAKER SECTION planners were taking no chances of another communication failure.[10]

The logistical plan, after the four phases had been completed, was to constantly resupply the operational base each third or fourth day. The personnel already on the ground would scout out different DZ locations within the bowl area where the initial DZ was for the follow-on drops, including resupply. The frequency of flights into this area, although at a distance from the nearest enemy troops, and in defilade with the hills and mountains in the immediate area could not screen enemy radar from the flyover approaches to the Sat'ae area indefinitely. Over a period of time the enemy analysis of their radar sightings certainly alerted them to suspect unusual airborne activity. Competent and experienced radar operators, who know the area, can identify the radar signature of the type aircraft its radar sights, therefore, it is suspected that enemy attention to the SPITFIRE operational area may have developed before the second augmentation was dropped.[11]

The actual operation began at 2030 hours, 18 June 1951, when the C-47 carrying Captain Anderson and his pathfinders took off from K-3 airbase at Pusan and headed north. The drop occurred at about 2200 hours and the pathfinder team jumped onto the mountain bowl. The location of the DZ was absolutely no problem and the jump occurred as planned. (The mission controller was circling the area in the C-47 and a few minutes after the jump he was advised via voice radio by Sgt. Miles that all had landed successfully except Captain Anderson who suffered from injuries to his back when he landed. Further, Miles advised that Anderson was in considerable pain, however the DZ was clean so they should proceed with the supply drop.) The bundles landed right on the DZ and except for Captain Anderson's injury the operation had been successful. After the supply drop, the decision was made to wait until dawn to recover bundles since a chance of compromise might occur if they started searching for the bundles using their flashlights. At early dawn all bundles and parachutes were recovered and buried. Excess equipment was also concealed. Captain Anderson states in his book, <u>BANNER OVER PUSAN</u>, that the time required to secure the parachutes and bundles, required more physical effort by the men and delayed their schedule. With the DZ cleared of any evidence of the drops, the pathfinder team moved up the mountain to select a base camp.[12]

After settling in at the base camp, a reconnaissance party checked the area and determined the absence of any activity by enemy forces or the local populace. Sgt. Garner reported to headquarters via radio on the morning of 19 June. His report contained a description of the DZ, the location of a new DZ for LIGHTENING to use, as well as a revised drop date of D+2. Captain Anderson's condition had worsened so Garner also requested that Anderson be evacuated from the area on the 22nd of June. The headquarters accepted the new drop date for LIGHTENING and instructed the pathfinders to conduct a reconnaissance of the area between their plateau and the town of Karyoju-Ri. While conducting the reconnaissance, the team met a Korean woodcutter who told them a North Korean army patrol had conducted a check of the hill above Karyoju-ri that morning but were no longer in the area. The North Koreans allegedly told the woodcutter that they had captured four South Korean parachutists east of the town the evening of 18 June. Miles via radio advised Anderson and Garner as well as the headquarters and also instructed headquarters to delay the drop of LIGHTENING. This incident varies from Captain Anderson's comments in his book, <u>BANNER OVER PUSAN</u>, where he states a young Korean, a resident of the area, was discovered by the team. This young man named Kim stated he hid out in the woods to avoid military service in the North Korean forces and he would aid them in locating secure base sites as well as leading them to enemy troop dispositions. After a while, the youth was permitted to visit his mother who lived in the area, but Kim never returned. Assuming this is true Kim may have led the North Korean forces into the area where they located all the caches of supplies and equipment SPITFIRE members had secured for later use.[13]

After completing the reconnaissance, Miles advised Anderson the area was clear and it was safe for LIGHTENING to make their jump. Sgt. Garner notified headquarters to make the drop at 0130 hours, June 23 and a flight path was to be northeast, a light will be displayed in the center of the DZ. The evacuation of Captain Anderson was also requested at this time for 0800 hours June 23, via helicopter.

While plans were in the process for LIGHTENING to drop, Sgt. Miles reported his sighting of a Chinese army division. The Chinese cleverly moved under cover of darkness then at daybreak would conceal troop units in side valleys or thick vegetation from UN airstrikes. Miles continued reporting his observations with resulting airstrikes by UN forces. His activities between 20-23 June triggered successive airstrikes against these Chinese units. Miles decided the Chinese must realize by now there were observers in the area reporting their positions, so he decided to move the pathfinder group and also delay the LIGHTENING augmentation drop. On the evening of 23 June Sgt. Garner made contact with Eight Army and arranged for a helicopter to come in at dawn and evacuate Captain Anderson and the Interpreter Song who developed a severe stomach illness. The evacuation was completed without any difficulty. The pathfinder team moved to BAKER, a site north of the plateau.[14]

LIGHTENING-the first augmentation that had been delayed jumped at 0130 hours June 26 on a new DZ that was a clearing on Sat'ae Mountain's eastern slope. Sgt. Miles provided guidance from the DZ to the aircraft crew on ground wind speed and direction with the center of the DZ marked by a bright flashlight. The drop was made off target so the jumpers landed on the eastern slope of the mountain, almost a mile away. Lt. Adams-Acton landed on rocks but was just shaken up. The Koreans landed in trees on the mountain slope and although bruised were not injured. The cargo bundles were scattered along a quarter-mile line. The bundles were not recovered until well after daylight. Since the Koreans had tree landings, it took some time to recover the personnel chutes and bury them. The augmentation group headed for BAKER on the plateau while Miles and Ho stayed behind. The magnitude of supplies and equipment made it necessary to secure them in the vicinity of the DZ for later use. Miles and Ho did that chore.[15]

While Miles and Ho secured the resupply drop material, the other members of LIGHTENING moved to the base site. The following morning they moved again, this time to the initial operation base on the plateau. Until the 30th of June, the group observed small units moving, not the same size as observed earlier by Sgt. Miles. On 30 June a resupply drop was made containing food, drugs and miscellaneous items, but again disaster struck because none of the cargo chutes deployed and each bundle was practically destroyed. A check of the cargo chutes revealed that the break-cord was made of flimsy twine, which broke prematurely and failed to pullout the cargo chute for deployment. There is no record as to how this failure was allowed to happened - sabotage or stupidity? The group expended considerable time collecting the debris from the area of the crashed bundles and then burying the material to avoid their discovery by any observers moving through the area.[16]

To further complicate the mission and most likely pinpointed the location to enemy forces was the action of the pilot of the resupply mission. On the night of 5-6 July, although the DZ was well marked and illuminated by flashlights, the pilot did not pick up the DZ. After circling the area repeatedly the pilot returned to base, refueled and came back to the DZ. His return was at 0400 hours with about one hour of darkness remaining. After being told by Sgt. Miles to leave the area, the pilot circled around until daybreak then made the drop, but over the base not the DZ. The following description of actions that occurred after the daylight resupply drop is based upon my interviews with former Sgt. Marvin G. Garner. Garner is the sole living survivor of Operation SPITFIRE. He is a retired teamster who presently resides in Alaska.

Garner who was the CW Radio operator admits that he remained by the ANGRC-9 radio to monitor incoming traffic as well as to transmit any traffic passed on to him by the team members. He does recall that after setting up the base camp initially a new face, a Korean appeared in camp. This Korean led the team into an area on a hillside where there was cover and concealment as well as access to water. It is believed this young Korean was the woodcutter the team met in the forest after jumping into the area. Garner describes the base camp as in a wooded area on a hillside. There was no structure or cave used by the team. Garner stated he had limited knowledge of what the other team members were actually engaged in when outside the base camp.

On the morning of July 6, after the daylight air resupply drop, Garner remained at his radio post while the other team members left the base camp area to recover the bundles. Garner related that this resupply drop was to contain weapons and ammunition, etc for the expansion of SPITFIRE operations. Shortly after the team members left the base camp, Garner heard extensive small arms fire and explosions. Very quickly after hearing the firing, Lt. Hearn and Lt. Adams-Acton ran into the base camp and shouted to Garner to get out of the camp. It had been compromised and the Chinese soldiers had recovered the weapons from the bundles and were firing at the team members. Hearn, Adams-Acton and Garner immediately ran from the base camp and started climbing the hill away from the camp. Garner had initially strapped the radio to himself, but quickly learned he could not continue the climb with the heavy load, therefore, he discarded the radio, but kept the codebook and ciphers in his possession. Hearn and Adams-Acton did the same so they too could better move across country. They carried only their 45 caliber pistols and little else.

Garner has high praise for Lt. Hearn and his ability to lead the group south toward the friendly lines. He recalls that Lt. Adams-Acton, although a fine officer was inexperienced in such activities; whereas Hearn was a WWII veteran with OSS service.

Hearn, Adams-Acton and Garner moved across the hills in a southerly direction towards the friendly lines. Their movement was confined to the hours of darkness. They would find a wooded area to conceal themselves during the daylight, then start moving after darkness. On one occasion as they moved along a trail they heard lots of voices, and then realized they were moving right through a Chinese bivouac area. They kept their heads low and continued through the area until they cleared it. On several occasions Garner recalls being challenged by Chinese sentries. When this happened they changed their direction and kept moving. Even though they had essentially only the clothes on their backs, Garner does not recall any illness or injuries happening to them by virtue of the cross-country movement. One incident did cause injury to Lt. Adams-Acton, but not so serious to impair his mobility.

Garner describes one occasion when they were hiding in a wooded thicket during daylight. Lt. Hearn left the concealment to investigate a noise followed by Adams-Acton, then Garner. As Garner emerged from the thicket he observed Lt. Adams-Acton attempting to fire his 45 caliber pistol at a Chinese soldier. Later Adams-Acton told Garner that he could not fire the pistol due to his unfamiliarity with a pistol since his experience in the British Army was with a 38 caliber Revolver. By not firing his pistol, the Chinese soldier assaulted Adams-Acton with an entrenching shovel, striking the Lieutenant on the head Adams-Acton dropped his pistol and appeared to be dazed from the blow to his head. In the meantime, the Chinese soldier picked up the pistol and attempted to fire it, but could not. Garner grabbed Lt. Adams-Acton and they ran away from the scene, following Lt. Hearn who had already started running. At this time Garner looked up and observed a line of Chinese soldiers moving along the hilltop. The three continued running down towards the river they had observed earlier and concealed themselves by jumping into the river and hiding along its bank. They remained in the neck deep water the rest of the day until darkness. The Chinese continued to search the area without finding them.

Using the river as their guide towards friendly lines, the three found a Korean boat tied up to the shore. Now, they thought their transportation was solved. They loaded into the boat and cast off into the main stream only to have the boat promptly sink. Now up to neck deep water they swam back to shore and started the long walk again. Fortunately, since they carried only their 45 caliber pistol their swimming not hampered by any heavy objects.

After the contact with the Chinese soldier the remainder of the exfiltration was uneventful until they approached the friendly lines. Garner remembers they began to hear the artillery firing as they came within range of frontline activity. Also during the darkness, they guided on the searchlights they observed. During the Korean War, the US Army adopted a procedure to employ searchlights that were mounted on tanks and would be directed at night towards the clouds causing a reflection over the battlefield. In that way, they could observe enemy movement on the front and respond to it. With these beacons of light, Garner said they could then more confidently move directly towards the friendly frontlines. As they closed near the lines, they began to shout "We are Americans do not shoot!" This obviously influenced their recognition by the US Infantrymen and they gained safe passage through the lines.

When asked about food supply during the exfiltration, Garner explained that Lt. Hearn would slip into the Korean kitchens, late at night, and steal whatever foodstuffs that he could find. The Korean houses are structured so that the kitchen is separate from the main sleeping structure. Therefore affording access to it at night without alerting the family. The food consisted of grain, rice, meat scraps whatever the family had left over from the previous food preparation.

After reaching the friendly frontlines, Garner explains that the three were turned over to Army Intelligence personnel at I Corps where they were immediately debriefed on enemy sightings and/or other data on the Chinese or N. Korean forces they had observed. Once those debriefings were completed, they were sent to Pusan where the 8th Army Miscellaneous Group (BAKER SECTION) was located.

While at the Miscellaneous Groups HQ. Garner said he met a colonel, possibly Colonel McGee, he does not recall the name. The Colonel asked him a few questions about the operations, but when Garner told the Colonel about the first helicopter flying in daylight over their base camp area and not sighting them for the pickup of Captain Anderson, therefore requiring a second helicopter flight that did find them and took out Anderson, the Colonel exploded with a few choice words and stormed out of the room. Garner never saw him again. Within a day of so after that meeting, the Miscellaneous Group sent Garner back to his unit. He was never subjected to a formal debriefing.
Garner being a very practical man said he assumed the debriefers did not think he could contribute anything to what Hearn and Adam-Acton would provide. He does not know if either of them was ever debriefed. So without a thank you or goodbye Sgt. Garner returned to his Signal Corps Unit for the duration of his tour in Korea.

There are two people in this story that standout due to their particular prior experience before joining operation SPITFIRE. In the case of 2d Lt. Adams-Acton he was fine well-educated graduate of the British Military Academy of Sandhurst. He also spoke fluent Chinese and could certainly contribute to the mission by virtue of language fluency. However, he was not experienced in either airborne or guerrilla operations and it showed up during the land exfiltration phase. According to Garner, if Lt. Hearn had not been there he felt the other two would not have made it. Lt. Hearn seemed to know just what to do at the moment something had to be decided. This is in no way an attempt to denigrate Lt. Adams-Acton; we all know experience certainly counts. I feel volunteering for a mission for which he had absolutely no knowledge or experience reflects his fearlessness.

Garner was in a completely different situation, except for the uncommon devotion to duty that both Adams-Acton and Garner demonstrated. Garner was from the state of Washington. He went into the US Army at the end of World War II and saw duty for a short time in Europe. He was subsequently discharged. When the Korean War began, Garner enlisted in the US Army Enlisted Reserve. Later he volunteered for active duty. He arrived in Korea in 1951 and was assigned to the 304th Signal Service Battalion as a Continuous Wave (CW) operator. As he recalls, one day a notice appeared on the bulletin board asking for radio operators to volunteer for a classified mission. Garner volunteered and was sent to Pusan to join the 8th Army Miscellaneous Group. He then learned he must make a parachute jump behind the lines with a group of US/British and Korean partisans. Garner was not airborne qualified so the Pusan element briefed him on jumping and then he made one practice jump. I think it takes lots of personal courage and belief in one's superiors that they know what they are doing to go on this mission. The personal courage was demonstrated, the professional knowledge of his superiors is in doubt. Although alluded to in this book already, one can only question the wisdom to conduct this operation from its beginning. In any event, this led to the demise of the 8th Army Miscellaneous Group and its activities were transferred to the 8240th Army Unit for a new beginning.

There appears no doubt that the combination of the two helicopter flights into the area of operations to bring out Captain Anderson coupled with the repeated flights by the C-47 culminating with the daylight airdrop of bundles over the base camp compromised the operation. The fact that the Chinese forces almost immediately recovered this last airdrop of the arms and ammunition leads one to believe the earlier helicopter flights influenced the Chinese focus on the area. The daylight airdrop cinched its compromise.

The survivors without any prior preparation were confronted with the challenge of safely reaching friendly lines about seventy miles away. Their circuitous route to evade the enemy would entail a journey of about 100 miles lasting about ten days. Led by lst Lt. David Hearn the journey was successfully made crossing into friendly the lines of the 35th Infantry Regiment

As alluded to earlier in this book, this failure along with other airborne delivery failures greatly influenced the transfer of this activity to the 8240th Army Unit. While BAKER SECTION was to stand down, AVIARY inherited all the forthcoming clandestine airborne operations. Although recognizing the failure of this operation to accomplish its planned mission, the location and calling in airstrikes that undoubtedly caused the death and major destruction of a Communist Chinese Army Division, must also be recognized as a singular accomplishment that no doubt kept hundreds of additional Communist Chinese troops from ever opposing the UN/US force.

AVIARY'S FIRST GREAT LOSS:

Although AVIARY had been conducting numerous successful airdrops of agents and their resupply, its luck ran out on February 18,1952. The scheduled mission called for agent drops in multiple locations of both Korean and Chinese volunteers. The area of the drop zones were around the port city of Wonsan on the east coast. Three DZs were involved with two agents dropped on each DZ. One DZ was west of the city, the second was north of the city and the third was north of the city but closer to Hungnam. Operation BIG BOY in the Wonsan area was to mark the DZ for the first drop with signal fires and flashlights. BIG BOY was a partisan team already operating in the Wonsan area.

At approximately 0145 hours, 19 February 1952, the C-46 aircraft of the 6153d Airbase Squadron based in Japan took off for the mission. According to the survivors who became prisoners of war, the flight to the first DZ was uneventful, the DZ was quickly identified by the displayed ground signals, so the pilot circled back to approach the DZ at a low jump altitude. The first two agents were moved towards the door and prepared to jump. The first agent jumped and was immediately followed by the second jumper, however, as the second agent exited the door he threw an active grenade into the aircraft. The explosion apparently blew the 8240th jumpmaster M/Sgt. Davis T. Harrison clear of the aircraft, since he was standing at the edge of the door. Pilot Captain Lawrence E. Burger, also liaison officer to the 8240th who remained at the controls of the critically damaged plane was killed when the plane crashed. Corporal George Tatarakis, the assistant jumpmaster was also near the door. It is assumed that Tatarakis was also blown from the aircraft or jumped quickly after the explosion. Harrison stated during his debriefing that he observed another parachute about two to three hundred yards up the flight path and above his position. It was his assumption that the parachute he saw was Tatarakis' because the flight crew members had more of a delay in exiting the plane and jumped very close to each other resulting in tighter landing pattern. After the crash, but before access to Harrison and the repatriated air crews, agents in the area reported sightings of a captured caucasian from the crashed aircraft being turned over by the North Koreans to Soviet officials. A former POW who had been held in Wonsan reported he had seen another American POW in the jail with a Greek sounding name who had shouted out from his cell that he was being taken to Russia. Since that time no further information on the fate of Tatarakis has surfaced [2]

The explosion killed all the other four agents aboard the aircraft along with Pfc. Dean H. Crabb who served as the contact with the agents. The North Korean officials later told the captured air crewmen that they found four Chinese agents, and the Americans, Crabb and Captain Burger, all dead aboard the plane. The air crewman as they exited the plane reported they observed the four agents and Crabb still strapped in their seats. The aircrew also suffered from the explosion. Staff Sergeant Rowden, radio operator was seriously wounded and was moved to the jump door by SSgt. Poldervaart who pulled Rowden's rip cord and his own as they jumped. The remaining crewmembers Lt. Layer, Captain King, Lt. Dick, and Lt. Haley managed to jump while Captain Burger remained at the controls and did his best to steady the aircraft until all the others had jumped. [3]

The jumpers were almost immediately captured by North Koreans and moved to prison camps for interrogation. It should be noted that M/Sgt. Harrison became the resolute leader in his camp to influence resistance to interrogations by the North Koreans. For his leadership while a prisoner of war he was recognized and awarded the Bronze Star.

As a result of this incident greater security was observed while conducting an AVIARY MISSION. The AVIARY jumpmasters insisted on checking the agents or partisans' weapons to ensue they were not loaded, that their ammunition supply was secured in such manner it could not be accessed during the flight. Additionally, grenades were secured in the same manner so the indigenous personnel would not be able to endanger the aircraft or its crew. I recall talk around the headquarters that Chinese radio or message transmissions were, in fact, intercepted that revealed what had happened to the aircraft but not in detail. So the tighten security measures were taken. I was also confronted with a similar security problem that is addressed in the description of a B-26 airdrop operation.[4]

This loss hit the AVIARY and the Airforce. Where AVIARY lost two Americans, assuming Tatarakis was killed, one prisoner of war, and six agents, the Airforce lost one gallant pilot and six airmen were captured.

The first clandestine airborne mission for me occurred on the same evening as the ill-fated C-46 crash. Having arrived at the 8240th Army Unit in early January 1952, I was temporarily assigned as the S-1, pending the arrival of an Adjutant General Branch officer to fill that position. Colonel Ives, the Commanding Officer, assured me that I would then go to AVIARY. In late January 1952 I did participate in training jumps on the sand bar of the Han River and became familiar with AVIARY operations.

The evening of the 19th of February, I accompanied Captain Fred Slawson the current leader of AVIARY, on the first mission. The assignments were made based upon perceived danger. The two missions that evening were partisan drops at the city of Sakchu that was near the Yalu River. It was considered more dangerous than the six agent drops near Wonsan that required a rather shallow penetration of air space north of the bombline. The decision was for the officers to take the Sakchu mission; the enlisted men would take the Wonsan area. Unfortunately the act of an agent to destroy the plane could not have been anticipated.

SHOOTDOWN OF THE B-26:

Although the operation that led to the loss of a B-26, has been described as not an AVIARY mission I feel it was about as close to AVIARY as one could imagine. The mission was basically an aerial reconnaissance mission for a potential agent and/or partisan operation that went bad.[5]

I had been a long time friend of Lt. Col. William Lewis and had the opportunity to video tape his oral history for his family and the U.S. Army War College files. In his video tape Lewis relates how he was recruited for the mission and its execution that led to his imprisonment as a Prisoner of War. Lewis was initially assigned to the Eighth Army Ranger Company and posted to the partisan base on Pyaengyang-do. While on the island he was approached by a representative of the CIA and asked of his potential interest in an attempt to rescue Major General Dean who had been captured by the North Koreans early in the war. Lewis was interested in the assignment with the CIA, so naturally he indicated he would like to participate in such an endeavor.

On September 16th, 1951, Lewis flew from Paengyang-do to Pusan and met with General Richard Stilwell, then a Colonel on detail to the CIA. It seemed that the CIA had traced General Dean while in captivity to a suspected prison camp near Ha-ri, northeast of Pyongyang, North Korea. The concept of the rescue featured only the General, not the other prisoners that may be there. There was some discussion of Lewis joining the CIA after his Korean tour, but the discussions centered on the rescue. Lewis indicated he would like to make an aerial reconnaissance of the prison camp and also pinpoint some possible drop zones adjacent to the camp.

With the interview completed, Lewis traveled to Taegu to personally request a B-26 aircraft through the good graces of Lt. Col. Koster, the commander of the Miscellaneous Group that controlled the BAKER SECTION operations. Initially, the talks fell on deaf ears, as Koster was not disposed to granting the request. Lewis had been sworn to secrecy as to the mission and could not discuss it even with Koster. Lewis in desperation finally posed the potential for a large partisan operation in that area and needed to make the aerial reconnaissance. Koster accepted this explanation and checked on aircraft availability. He told Lewis that Captain Hearn of BAKER SECTION had a scheduled flight in a B-26 to make his own aerial reconnaissance of potential DZs near Wonsan. Koster then called the Airforce and asked that the flight stop at Taegu and pickup Lewis. As requested the B-26 landed at Taegu early on the morning of September 17, the pilot Major Wright, navigator Fred Pelser and Captain Hearn joined Lewis for a briefing on his area of interest.

The pilot understood and the navigator plotted their course to proceed from Taegu out over the Sea of Japan to climb over the east coast mountain range near Wonsan. They would recon the area, and then proceed northwest to Ha-Ri just inland from the west coast and north of Pyongyang. Lewis and Hearn had worked together earlier and were good friends. The first recon near Wonsan was over an area previously used by a MUSTANG team. The initial recon was completed without incident and the B-26 headed towards Lewis' area of interest near the west coast. The reconnaissance was conducted around the town of Ha-Ri then the pilot asked if Lewis had seen enough. Lewis replied he had. The pilot advised over the intercom he had only a few rounds of 50 caliber machine gun ammunition left as the plane climbed to about 4000 feet of altitude.

According to Lewis, he then heard the pilot over the intercom say "That SOB is shooting at us!" Lewis asked, "Where?" The pilot said, "You'll see." The B-26 then rolled over and went into a steep dive Lewis and Hearn were seated in the Plexiglas nose of the plane and could see everything in front and just below the front of the aircraft. Lewis described the scene; they observed the single, antiaircraft gun position and the numerous red balls of flak passing by them. Lewis felt if they had flown perhaps a few seconds further the antiaircraft fire would have missed the plane. Lewis felt the hit between the front nose position and the cockpit. The intercom went out and hissing noises of the broken hydraulic system could be heard. At this time, Lewis looked back towards the cockpit. He could see it through the tunnel that extended from the cockpit to the nose of the plane. Lewis saw what he thought was pair of legs disappear upwards, that was probably the navigator's legs. Hearn then released the nose hatch and he and Lewis bailed out. The hatch cover did not completely free itself so it was difficult to

41

squeeze out of the plane. Pelser later while in prison with Lewis told him he observed the B-26 clearing the mountaintop with a pair of legs dangling out the nose of the plane. Lewis said he thought that they were his legs because he bailed out as soon as he saw the crew abandoning the plane.[6]

Lewis and Pelser were the only survivors. The pilot and Captain Hearn were killed most likely due to bailing out at such an extremely low altitude with no time for the parachute to deploy. Although this was an aerial reconnaissance mission, its cover was the fact that the B26 carried bombs and its guns were fully charged so bombing and strafing actions could be done to cover its true purpose. The B-26 was known for its hit and run tactics against targets of opportunity. I recall one such mission, at night with low-level runs against enemy truck convoys. When the aircraft landed at K-16 it had clothes lines wrapped around its tail.[7]

A word about both Lewis and Pelser are in order as to their preparation for this fateful mission. In a telephone interview with Pelser he described his assignment to this mission. In the early morning hours of September 16, Pelser had just returned from a B-26 armed mission over North Korea. As he headed to the billets, he was asked by operations if he would take the September 17 mission, departing about 0800 hours. The mission was to be merely an aerial reconnaissance and hits on targets of opportunity. Pelser agreed and turned in for what was left of the morning. At about 0730, the operations representative came to his room to wake him since he had failed to report for the morning flight. Pelser dressed immediately and went to operations.

Pelser had not eaten since breakfast on the 16th of September and on this morning did not have time to eat before takeoff. At the time of capture Pelser had not eaten for about eighteen hours, a hell of a way to go into a Korean prison. While a prisoner, Pelser supported Lewis' cover story and claimed ownership of a plastic relief map Lewis had taken with him to plot DZs. Pelser deserves recognition as a true hero who fortunately survived the ordeal.[8]

Lewis went on the mission wearing his Class A, khaki uniform with ribbons and jump wings as well as the Eighth Army patch with an airborne-ranger tab. Lewis realizing he could be compromised with the patches and insignias began removing them as he evaded capture after landing so by the time he was captured they had been removed and buried. His cover story that he was running a rest and recuperation camp in Korea coupled with the khaki uniform probably supported the cover story. He told the interrogators that his cousin, the deceased pilot, offered him an adventurous flight and he accepted. The Koreans evidently felt Lewis was stupid for doing such and initially accepted the story.

However Lewis' luck ran out after Adams-Acton arrived in the same prison camp and inadvertently compromised Lewis. The Koreans then really worked over Lewis for some time. It seems Adams-Acton, of the earlier SPITFIRE operation, and others in the US operational headquarters had assumed that Lewis had been killed in the B-26 crash. Adams-Acton had been captured with partisan forces on Tae HWwa-Do, so the Koreans knew he was with Special Operations. Adams -Acton later explained to Lewis that he felt he had to tell the Korean something so he talked about Lewis.[9]

Fortunately Lewis and Pelser survived in the prison camp and were returned after the cease-fire. In my temporary duties as the S-1, I reviewed files in the 8240th Headquarters and found tidbits of information about Captain Hearn, but nothing regarding Bill Lewis. The author developed and submitted an award of the Silver Star for

Captain Hearn based upon his previous activities on operation SPITFIRE. There was no information about the B-26 shootdown in the 8240th Headquarters. It is assumed that the BAKER SECTION and the Eighth Army Miscellaneous Group's files were in such disarray, the information about the B-26 shootdown was lost. When video taping Bill Lewis he said he had been advised, by someone he could not recall, that an award of the Bronze Star had been submitted on him. Based upon my experience it seems that the award was never submitted.

Over fifty years later and in the present day technological environment it is postulated that a mission such as the B-26 Aerial Reconnaissance would not have been done. Also it is difficult to critique failures of this mission unless one mentally approaches such critique with comparisons of that day's experience and capability to conduct such operations. I, having been in the middle of such activity, for an extended period, feel some observations are in order.

First, the mission seemed to be the conceptualization of the CIA staff and if successful a great morale booster for the United States, especially its troops in Korea. The speed in which the operation developed " legs" is questionable. Recall only General Stilwell, the CIA operative on Pyongyang-Do and Bill Lewis apparently knew the purpose of Lewis' reconnaissance, thereby compartmenting Lewis from seeking detailed briefings and conducting a map and aerial photo reconnaissance, before flying into the area. AVIARY personnel always consulted the Airforce operations staff for detailed information on antiaircraft gun positions or observer stations, as well as information about other aircraft activities in the area that might influence the ground observers. The B-26 flight was just that, and not a prelude to a clandestine airborne operation.

For Lewis, the haste in going on this mission leads one, again, to feel there was inadequate planning and coordination of intelligence about the target. The physical condition of the navigator who had not had adequate rest, not even a meal for the prior eighteen hours and essentially hustled aboard this flight with what appears to be inadequate knowledge of the area, especially its antiaircraft defenses. Evidence of this haste is the fact he was still wearing his Class A Khaki uniform no survival gear or weapon. However, one must credit the initiative of Lewis and the cooperation of Pelser in initially making Lewis' cover story work. One could conclude that the American soldiers' "Can Do" attitude, especially in wartime, often influences a rush to please, a rush to accomplish the task, but quite often results in disaster.

USE OF THE B-26 BOMBER AND THE COMMUNIST AIR DEFENSE:

BAKER SECTION and AVIARY when planning a clandestine airborne mission, based on current intelligence data available on potential DZs, would make a recommendation on the type aircraft they considered most suitable for the specifics of the mission. Obviously, if the type aircraft desired was not available, the planning would be revised to adjust for the type aircraft available. For single or small teams of agents and/or partisans flying into a "hot" area, especially for DZs in or near "MIG" alley, the B-26 was the most capable. It had the load capacity for small teams, the speed and capability to evade ground fire and possibly attacking enemy aircraft. The B-26, even while transporting personnel in its bombay, still had charged 50 caliber machine guns to defend itself or hit targets of opportunity. This capability afforded a defense for the aircraft and a plausible cover story for the B-26 being in the particular area.

I had such a mission in early June, 1952. The mission required the aerial delivery of two North Korean agents on a DZ that was located just northeast of the city of Pyongyang. The map and aerial photograph studies revealed several potential DZs. The requirement from the agents' handler was to make the drop as close in to the city as possible, yet as secure as possible. Both agents knew the area very well and indicated they could easily locate themselves and move into the city from the north or northeast quadrant.

The DZ selected was on the northeast side of the city in a hillside clearing so the aircraft could approach from the northeast flying below the immediate hill mass, as well as the mountain range that was east of the range of hills. This approach would provide a screen from radar, a low altitude approach of about 600 feet, and the aircraft could continue the low altitude mode for a few minutes before climbing to great altitude then turning east to cross over the east coast mountain range.[1]

The organization for the mission was as follows; I would fly in the softnose (plexiglas bubble) with the navigator, Lt. Gardner, the assistant jumpmaster, Corporal Carver, would be seated in the Bombay between the two agents equipped with a headset to maintain communications with the crew. Captain Black, the pilot, had flown several AVIARY missions as well as Lt. Gardner so there was no apprehension of missing the target DZ. The flight took off from K16 at approximately 2300 hours with a flight time of about two hours plus. The flight route was to fly over the Sea of Japan parallel to the east coast, then cross into North Korean airspace well north of Hungnam and over the mountain range, then drop to a defilade altitude using the mountains and hillmass to avoid enemy radar sightings. The flight then proceeded on a northwestern course until it was due north of the DZ and still flying at extremely low altitude. The approach to the DZ was at an altitude of about 600 feet. The navigator and I compared the ground features with the plastic relief map we held on our laps and agreed on the selected DZ[2]

About four minutes out, the pilot and navigator agreed on the heading, altitude and speed. Corporal Carver was advised by me on the intercom that the Bombay door would open immediately and to punch the two agents in the side to alert them. Carver acknowledged the task and reported the Bombay doors were fully opened. Within seconds I ordered the jump to commence and the agents dropped from the plane. The pilot then advised Carver to watch his legs as the doors were closing. The personnel jumping from a B-26 had to seat themselves on the wooden bench and then raise their legs over the doors as they closed and then reverse the procedure as the doors opened. Actually, personnel in the Bombay rested their legs on the closed doors while in flight.

With the drop completed, the pilot continued in the same flight mode for a few seconds or minutes and then began to climb to a higher altitude. Almost immediately, the plane was completely illuminated by searchlights. The pilot advised on the intercom to hold on as he began to take evasive action. The plane would twist, turn and dive at maximum speed to avoid the searchlights. The navigator and I were simply amazed at the degree of illumination the searchlights provided. It was possible to clearly read the map from that illumination. The navigator was viewing the map and advising the pilot at the same time. As the plane broke contact, one could observe the searchlights spinning around in all directions, then suddenly all were focused on the plane. This happened several times until the pilot followed a heading essentially, back along the approach followed before for the drop. By finally dropping into defilade with the hillmass in the background the radar lost its sighting of the aircraft. The action over Pyongyang happened so fast that the antiaircraft guns began firing at the aircraft just minutes before radar contact was lost.[3]

Although not officially confirmed I believe this was one of the first radar controlled integrated air defense contacts where searchlights were used against these classified UN flights. I recall that the AVIARY missions scheduled for the next day and all north of the bombline flights were canceled. There was a twenty-four hour standdown to allegedly checkout an unaccounted aircraft loss by Fifth Airforce.

My suspicion that the foregoing account of the first encounter with the Soviet built air defense system seems to be supported by information reported by Robert F. Futrell. This Airforce historian in his article, **"The United States Airforce In Korea," 1950-1953"**, Office of Air Force History, Washington, D.C. 1983, Futrell discusses the incident on June 10-11, 1952 regarding the loss of five B-29 Bombers over Kwaksan, North Korea. He states that, "Beginning in June 1952, when they (Communists) established their ground-control intercept capability, the Communists worked hard to counter the Superfortress raids". In addition he states, "After June, 1952 FEAF actively pushed electronic countermeasures. The 548th Reconnaissance Technical Squadron added a section that collated, evaluated, and disseminated electronic data obtained by 91st Squadron "ferret aircraft."

Regarding the B-26 flights, Futrell quotes BG William P. Fisher, USAF stating " In night flights at lower altitudes, the Fifth Air Force's B-26's were able to escape most of the hazards of the Red night air defenses, but the Superforts proved extremely vulnerable to the Communists air defense system". Fortunately, for the mission just described, the B-26 was available for that mission and proved what General Fisher stated about the evasive capability of the B-26.

Missions in the unarmed, larger aircraft, and their slow speed, the C-46 and C-47 troop carrier aircraft still was the prime source for these clandestine airborne missions. It was therefore, extremely important for the AVIARY mission planners to maintain an awareness of enemy air defense capabilities as well as their fighter aircraft activities. General Fisher again quoted in Futrell's article points out that the enemy had "an extremely well-developed ground-control radar interception capability over northwestern Korea, particularly within a 90-mile radius of Antung. Anywhere north of the Chongchon River the Reds had enough searchlights to pick up and illuminate night-flying B-29s." In addition to the radar control interception system, while flying in the C-46 or C-47, their vulnerability was to enemy aircraft in those areas mention by General Fisher. An effort was always made to contact the Navy Nightcap flights in the area for help in case a bogey appeared. This actually happened on a C-46 flight piloted by Captain Richard Armellino. He was advised via radio by a Nightcap fighter pilot that a bogey was on a rear approach, but then called back and advised that he had taken care of the bogey. Everyone aboard the aircraft breathed with a sign of relief and great praise for the Navy pilot.[4]

One final comment on the use of the B-26, for resupply drops. I decided to take on a resupply mission that again was in the northwestern quadrant, west of Pyongyang. The mission was a simple resupply drop of one fairly large bundle that could be accommodated in the Bombay. I was flying again with pilot, Captain Black, and navigator T. Gardner. I seated myself in the Bombay, on the wooden platform that had been secured in the Bombay. The platform was placed forward in the Bombay allowing adequate space between the rear edges of both the platform and the Bombay for the bundle to drop out. The bundle had been secured, and the static line hooked to the bomb shackle. The position in the Bombay is likened to sitting in a sewerline with no outside view until the Bombay doors open. The headset for intercom use is the link to the outside world. Should something happen to the aircraft that prevents the doors from opening comes to the forefront of your mind. In this case, the navigator found the DZ, the pilot advised he was opening the doors and the author should await the navigator's word to release the bundle. The drop was successful, With bundles it was also policy for the pilot to incline the aircraft slightly to aid in pushing the bundle off the platform. It was also very dangerous to accidentally let the cargo chute deploy prematurely because the drag of the chute can pull the bundle against the rear edge of the Bombay causing it to not drop clear of the aircraft. Should that happen the jumpmaster must advise the pilot to not close the doors and then work himself into a position where he can cut the chute lines, freeing the bundle. Naturally, while this is happening the aircraft is miles away from the DZ and the supplies are lost. Handling a B-26 drop required training and practice to ensure the jumpmaster was fully capable. Should the jumpmaster accidentally fall from the aircraft he would use the airforce type parachute with ripcord.

As General Fisher pointed out in his observations regarding aerial operations north of the bombline, the B-26 bombers worked were effective in their night intruder attacks against the North Korean infrastructure such as rail cuts, road destruction, power facilities troop concentrations as well as enemy vehicular traffic. On many of the B-26 missions, I observed from the nose position of the B-26 low-level attacks against long columns of vehicles moving along the main supply routes. In early 1952, one could tell when the personnel in the convoys heard the engines of the approaching aircraft, as the headlights began to fade out from front to rear of the column. However, beginning in the summer of 1952, it appeared the enemy convoy commanders were under orders to continue moving, even while under attack.

When planning a clandestine airborne operation, every effort was made to determine, during the pre-briefing, the locations of UN air missions near the area of the clandestine drop. Coordination was effected to first avoid blundering into a hot area unannounced and secondly to take advantage of the distraction the aerial attacks provided for the airdrop. On occasion, near a rail line cut, the air drop mission could have been compromised due to the million candlepower magnesium flares that were dropped through the night so repeated attacks could be made by the B-26s to prevent local manpower from immediately beginning repairs to the rail line cuts. The flares provided tremendous illumination of the area.[5]

GREEN DRAGON:

This is a very interesting and intriguing operation. It was the largest clandestine airborne partisan operation planned. The concept again called for the establishment of operational bases in North Korea that, if successful would facilitate expanded partisan presence and effectiveness in North Korea as well as provide a sustaining force capable of providing some defense against enemy actions. The team dropped on January 25, 1953 radio contact from GREEN DRAGON was not made until early March. The reports indicated personnel strengths had dropped from 97 to 31 partisans. There is no data to verify why the strength dropped by either desertions, killed or captured. Reports indicated there was sporadic radio contact over a six-month period, but under suspicion of being compromised.[1]

The mere size and its initial deployment leave one with reservations as to its potential for success. First, the DZ. was west of Pyongyang, near the village of Kokchang. This is a mountainous area about forty miles from Pyongyang. The large body of partisans with several hundred pounds of light infantry small arms and ammunition, grenades, etch was also dropped. The drop consisted of three, C-119 aircraft flying in five-minute intervals, beginning at approximately 2245 hours. In addition, a B-26 bomber was used as pathfinder; however, the terrain features were clearly visible to aid in pinpointing the location of the DZ. The flights did not encounter any antiaircraft fire (flak), however, automatic, small arms fire was observed by muzzle flashes coming from the ground.[2]

In April 1953, GREEN DRAGON reported the presence of five downed airmen. The headquarters approved another drop on 18/19 May of as many as 56 partisans and supplies. With great concern for the rescue of the alleged downed airmen, a decision was made to attempt a pickup using the Personnel Pick-up Ground Station. It was referred to by the airmen as the "snatch pick-up." In the summer of 1952, AVIARY jumpmasters with the Airfare team demonstrated the pick-up system in order to be knowledgeable of its requirements for deployment and its capability. The system required poles to be set up vertically on which nylon ropes would be aligned. The approaching aircraft would lower a line with a hook on the end to catch the nylon rope and the individual in the harness attached to the nylon rope would be almost immediately hoisted from the ground. Although the lift up was very fast, the terrain must provide for a low and slow approach for the aircraft.[3]

The pick-up was scheduled for May 24, 1953. As described in Colonel Mike Haas's book, **IN THE DEVIL'S SHADOW, UN SPECIAL OPERATIONS DURING THE KOREAN WAR,** one of the downed pilots Lt. Gilbert L. Ashley who was on the ground, verified to the B flight pilot that everything was set for the pick-up so the fifty pound "snatch bundle" was dropped. After assurance from Lt. Ashley that the pick-up system was in position, the pilot Major David M. Taylor started his approach. However, when his aircraft was hit by automatic small arms fire, Taylor recalls instead of seeing the vertical poles of the snatch bundle he observed 50 caliber machine guns firing at his aircraft. The mission was abruptly aborted. The five downed airmen were not returned by the North Koreans and were, therefore, declared dead by the United States.

In considering the manner and the time taken to conduct the drop of the initial group coupled with the knowledge that enemy small arms fire had been encountered during the drop there was every reason to assume the operation had been compromised. The spotty radio contacts and extended delays between contacts was sufficient to declare this operation compromised from the start. There is no data to show if a parallel intelligence operation was run to reestablish the bona fides of the initial group before anymore personnel or supplies were dropped. This may have been a case of right hand not communicating with the left?

OPERATION BLUEBOY:

There was an element within the Special Operations type units organized by the General Headquarters, Far East Command, at the behest of General Almond, then Chief of Staff, that conducted tactical intelligence collection operations. Although generally employed to support the front-line troops units, including the GHQ Raider Company and the Special Activities Battalion, this collection element became known as OPERATION BLUEBOY. When the hostilities basically stabilized the frontlines and the Xth Corps adjusted itself into the Eighth US Army on its eastern flank. These special type units were deactivated, except for the collection element. OPERATION BLUEBOY then became part of the 8240th Army Unit known as the Far East Command Liaison Detachment.

The mission of the Blueboy operatives was to continue its tactical intelligence collection activities along the Xth Corps front. To accomplish this mission BLUEBOY employed two means of infiltration of enemy lines. The first and the one BLUEBOY was experienced in was the use of indigenous line-crossers. The infiltrators would cross enemy lines, up to twenty- thirty miles, establish observation positions, collect intelligence information and return by ground exfiltration through enemy lines as well as friendly lines with their information. Many of these agents reported that the most dangerous portion of their exfiltration was crossing back into friendly lines. Quite often these agents were killed by front-line troops before their identification could be made known, others were captured, reported as a prisoner of war and actually processed through prisoner of war holding areas until their agent handler became aware of the capture and had them released. In one instance, when the prisoner of war capture rate was extremely low, an agent was processed all the way through the system to avoid embarrassing the unit commander who boasted about the capture rate for his particular unit.

The second means of operations was the air infiltration of agents beyond the limited ground infiltration distances so tactical intelligence collection operations could provide advance warning of enemy troop movements toward Xth Corps' front. Unlike the line-crossers, these agent teams included a radio operator with an ANGRC-9 radio with a continuous wave (CW) capability. Therefore, these teams remained in the enemy rear areas longer than the line-crossers, reported via radio and could be easily resupplied by air near their base of operations. I recall conducting several air drops of BLUEBOY agents as well as their resupply in areas east and south of Wonsan harbor. The area facilitated some good drop zones in the foothills of the Taebaek mountain range along the east coast. One difficulty was coordinating the delivery of the agents to AVIARY because it was based out of K-16 near Seoul, completely across the peninsula from BLUEBOY that was located on the east coast near Sokcho-Ri.

To improve operations, reduce downtime traveling between two locations and be more responsive to BLUEBOY, a small, unimproved airstrip that could accommodate a

48

C-47 aircraft was selected. The AVIARY mission would be accomplished by flying into this small airstrip in the early evening of the scheduled drop. The agents were briefed and then turned over to AVIARY jumpmasters only a few minutes before takeoff. The mission was flown and upon its completion, BLUEBOY was advised by AVIARY's headquarters. This coordination worked out very well for BLUEBOY, but the pilots did not care much for the airstrip, since it was very short, very rough and takeoff could be made only in the direction of the Sea of Japan. The landings were made only in daylight hours due to the airstrip's condition and its close proximity to the mountainous terrain that began close to the end of the airstrip.

Earlier in this book, I described the dropping of an intelligence collection team near Wonsan Harbor and the fact the team exfiltrated through the lines only after a few days. The team had not been given the crystals for the radio therefore they could not report their observations. This team was a BLUEBOY team and the mix-up probably occurred because headquarters failed to realize the team would not report to AVIARY in Seoul for the mission but would be picked up at their base in Sokcho-Ri. The team did have all its equipment for the mission except for the crystals. That team was subsequently dropped again on the same mission, but with their crystals. The US personnel with BLUEBOY were excellent to work with and enjoyed a good reputation among the UN frontline divisions with whom they worked. I was told by a former marine who was with the First Marine Division when it was in the Xth Corps that he observed a BLUEBOY agent making his way towards the main outpost line of the division one morning at daybreak. The agent stepped on a mine and lost his foot. Since he could neither be reached due to the minefield nor could he move, he placed his cap over his foot and sat there and bled to death. My friend was quite impressed on the dangers these agents faced and the courage they exhibited in performing their secret line-crossing missions.

COL Higgins, CO, FECLD; LTC Doupe, Dir., Intelligence; and LTC Vanderpool, Dir., Guerilla Division - 1952.

B-26 Bomber was assigned to Baker Flight for classified missions. Photographed at K-16, 1952.

Intelligence collection team ready to airdrop into North Korea.

Mr. John Hong jumped near Wonson Harbor in 1951. He exfiltrated lines, then worked with 24th ID TLO Team. Photograph courtesy of Mr. Hong.

North Korean Partisans worked with AVIARY on parachute jumps and line crossing operations with front line Divisions. All were qualified radio operators. Source: Mr. Lim, who jumped near Wonson Harbor in 1951.

Operation Spitfire

Three members of the 8086th MISC Group return from behind the Communist Lines. (L - R) SGT. Marvin G. Garner (Longview, Washington State), LT. Leo Adams-Acton (Hythe, Kent, England), LT. David Hearn (Cornith, Mississippi) point out Communist positions to CPT Chavez and LT Hassel on the map at G-2, I Corps near Uijongbu, Korea. US Army Photo by PFC. D. Hildreth, Photo Section - 51st Signal Battalion, Corps

Operation Spitfire

Three members of the 8086th AU MISC Group pose in front of G-2, US Corps after returning from behind Communist lines. (L - R) LT. Leo Adams-Acton (Hythe, Kent, England), LT. David Hearn (Cornith, Mississippi), and SGT. Marvin G. Garner (Longview, Washington State) G-2 Section, I Corps near Uijongbu, Korea. US Amy Photo by PFC. D. Hildreth, Photo Section - 51st Signal Battalion, Corps

CHAPTER VII

OVERALL REVIEW OF CLANDESTINE AIRBORNE OPERATIONS

The development of clandestine airborne operations expanded from the AVIARY agent operations with its first drop on September 26, 1950 when two flights containing a total of nine agents were dropped within the assumed paths of the retreating NKPA forces, as a result of the Inchon landing. The Eighth Army, along with Xth Corps needed this tactical information to inhibit the NKPA's withdrawal. These nine agents, one of which was Richard Hong of KLO found good positions to observe NKPA forces moving along the principal roads leading north. Without radios or other means to send their sightings in a timely manner to Eighth Army, therefore the mission was a failure. Eight of the agents returned through friendly lines. Hong resides in the United States today.[1]

The following AVIARY mission, although a simple collection of tactical intelligence, was just the reverse of the earlier combat conditions. The Chinese Communists Forces (CCF) entered the war and the UN Forces began withdrawing. The UN forces seriously needed order of battle information on the CCF. General Walker, Commanding General, US, Eighth Army desperately needed to predetermine possible points of attack the CCF may adopt against his forces. AVIARY's principal officer conceptualized a clandestine airborne operation to attack this contingency. His concept called for twelve teams of two men each, to jump into DZs located about twenty miles forward of the UN Outpost Line of Resistance (OPLR) across the entire width of the Korean peninsula. Since adequate radio equipment was still not available, the agents were issued colored smoke grenades they would use as a means of reporting. The vehicle to monitor these "smoke" reports was a C-47 aircraft that flew at mid-day over the line of DZs. The smoke signals were red if a CCF battalion size unit had been observed, yellow for North Korean units, and green would indicate observations of insignificant sized forces. This simple operation was a throwback to the days of Custer's 7th Cavalry and Indian smoke signals, but Lt. Brewer, of AVIARY reported a 25% success rate, despite reduced visibility as the weather conditions changed.[2]

An aside to this story is that most of these agents did not make more AVIARY operations, but joined the various Tactical Liaison Offices (TLO), actually known as "Line Crossers." Hong became a member of the 24th ID, TLO for the remainder of the war. Lt. Brewer was the officer in charge of AVIARY at its initiation and was plunged into these critical operations with little support. There was a tremendous lack of knowledge among his superiors as to how clandestine airborne operations should be planned and conducted. It is understandable in this fast moving combat environment the initial basic attempts to conduct these types of operations were very limited in success

Technical Memorandum ORO-T-64 (AFFE) dated June 1956 was published as part of. The post hostility study conducted by the Operations Research Office, Johns Hopkins University by a research team headed by Frederick W. Cleaver. The result of their review and analysis is an excellent source of information, especially the airborne portion, for historians and researchers.[3]

Their findings pertain principally to partisan clandestine airborne operations, but very little information on the agent drops. This may have been due to classifications where some agent operations still existed and might be compromised. It is important to note that hundreds of agent drops and their resupply missions occurred on a rather constant basis, while the partisan operations took more time to develop. The partisan operations became immediately dormant with the cease-fire. However to recount such partisan operations in period one, January to November 1951, as studied in the analysis, only two clandestine airborne operations with partisans were executed. These operations have been covered in the Selected Clandestine Airborne Operations Section. They were, of course, VIRGINIA I and SPITFIRE.[4]

In period two, December 1951 to April 1953, there were ten partisan clandestine airborne operations conducted. The reported total involvement was 38 teams that involved 394 partisans. Eight of these missions were attacks against the infrastructure, especially enemy rail or highway traffic (MSR), and two attempts to setup partisan bases.

Beginning in early 1952, the partisans were ready to start operations. Four teams were dropped on three different operations in the next series of partisan airborne missions. Contact was lost immediately with three of the teams, while one succeeded in destroying railroad tracks and attacking enemy facilities. I had been the jumpmaster on the successful team, Mustang IV that consisted of fifteen males and one female partisan. I recall the mission very clearly due to the presence of the female partisan, the large group, and the oversized equipment bundles that were to accompany them. The problem visualized was how to quickly execute the sixteen-person stick and also get the bundles out immediately behind them. A close landing pattern on the DZ influenced a quicker ground recovery of parachutes and equipment bundles, and movement away from the DZ. The solution was to raise the canvas bucket seats opposite the jump door side of the aircraft, move the bundles to a position just opposite the door, and leave enough space for the jumpers to pass. Once the last jumper started to exit the assistant jumpmaster and crew chief pushed the bundles toward the door so their exit from the aircraft was about at the same time interval between jumpers, which was a matter of seconds.[5]

I was quite interested in learning of this team's disposition after the drop. Later, I was informed that the team had conducted several attacks against enemy groups, had successfully damaged railroad lines and then exfiltrated to the off shore islands as their supplies had been expended and they did suffer causalities. The partisans made it to Tae-Hwda Do where Donkey-15 was based and where the Chinese intermittently launched attacks to sweep the partisans off those islands and neutralize the raids they had been conducting ashore. Although this certainly did not constitute a major success, it did give renewed vigor to the partisans and their US leaders to continue the struggle.

During June and July of 1952, 105 partisans volunteered for airborne training and subsequent missions. These volunteers were flown from Leopard Base, on Pyongyang-Do, to Seoul for basic airborne training. As head of AVIARY, I made arrangements to provide airborne training for a week in Seoul, followed by two practice jumps on the Han River sandbar. The partisans demonstrated a high state of morale and were attentive students. The training and practice jumps were completed without any difficulties. The return to Pyongyang-Do was a big thrill for the partisans because they jumped on the island for their comrades and some family members to see. It was reported that the Chinese headquarters reported an imminent partisan airborne invasion was anticipated.

The 105 partisans were flown in five, C-46 aircraft and the drops were made on single passes, following in line. The operations probably did appear to be on a large scale to the Chinese. No doubt this group of airborne qualified partisans comprised the major part of the GREEN DRAGON operation that came later.[6]

Additional clandestine airborne operations were conducted during the period fall of 1952 into the spring of 1953. The final MUSTANG RAIDERS missions were reported as being successful with each team destroying a train, even though contact was lost with headquarters. The teams were presumed to have been killed or captured. Team 7 was employed in extreme North Korea, not too far from the Yalu River while team 8 was employed in central North Korea, on a line between Hungnam on the east and Chongju on the west[7]

The code named JESSE JAMES teams, shown on the map as No. 9 to 11 simply vanished with no reporting as to whether they ever became operational. The objectives of these teams were to destroy infrastructure, especially railroad beds, trains, road cuts, and attacks on enemy forces. JESSE JAMES II and III, comprising of ten partisans each, jumped on the night of 27/28 December, while Team I was delayed until the evening of 29/30 December 1952 because of aircraft mechanical problems. The target area for these teams was the mountainous terrain southeast of Sariwon, but adjacent to the MSR and rail line between Pyongyang and Kaesong. None of these teams reported in after the jump. Again it had to be presumed they were killed or captured before becoming operational.[8]

Clandestine airborne partisan operations in 1952 had not been very productive. The airborne intelligence operations that dropped either a single agent or small groups of three to four agents did provide some successes. There continued to be success in agent recovery in the Xth Corps area where operation BLUEBOY was located. A series of low level order of battle (OB) intelligence collection missions were conducted. The airdrops were short "piston" like airspace penetrations. However, as the frontline stabilized and internal security measures were strengthened, the movement of agents within this frontline area became extremely difficult. There had been an ongoing observation and collection operation conducted in the area south of Wonson that provided OB information needed by Xth Corps units. As alluded to earlier in this book, radio crystals had not been provided to the team so its radio was useless. I dropped this same OB collection team on two occasions on DZs south of Wonson. On the first drop, after securing its gear and concealing the parachutes, the team started up the mountain trail and encountered a North Korean Army patrol. They exchanged greetings and mutually confirmed both elements were searching for suspected parachutists in the area. Their luck held. The team eventually, on orders, destroyed their equipment and exfiltrated through the lines.[9]

In 1953, the largest clandestine airborne partisan operation, GREEN DRAGON, was executed. This operation is covered in the section Selected Clandestine Airborne Operations. However, additional partisan airborne operations were also conducted such as the BOXER I, II, III, and IV. These 12 men teams were assigned the mission of destroying railroad lines connecting the Soviet Union and North Korea. The area of operations was between Songjin, North Korea, located less than fifty miles from Vladovostok, Siberia, and extending south to Hungham.[10]

I had made several agent and resupply drops in this area in 1952. . It was considered a "hot" spot, considering its proximity to the Soviet border. It was also known that the

52

Soviets based many of its air defense squadrons of MIGs in the Port city, therefore the threat of attack by MIGs and the effectiveness of Soviet radar, always concerned the pilots and jumpmasters when making this run.

The BOXER drops and DZs are listed for convenience of following the action:

BOXER I	Jumped on 6/7 February 1953	Near Yongdae-Ri
BOXER II	Jumped on 6/7 February 1953	Near Tong-Ni
BOXER III	Jumped on 8/9 February 1953	Near Tanch'On
BOXER IV	Jumped on 8/9 February 1953	Near Songjin

These teams dropped along a south to north line beginning north of the port city of Hungnam spaced about 20-30 miles apart. It was in the proximity of the east coast MSRs and. Songjin which was about fifty miles from the Soviet border. This again caused the planners to be extremely careful in avoiding a cross-border incursion by US aircraft. This operation had some success and there were no reported losses. The teams exfiltrated to the east coast and were picked up by the US Navy. In this operation, one can see the value in a hit and run focused objective along an extended area of exposed rail lines and the MSR. These types of operations were more successful than those that conceptualized the establishment of an operational base in North Korea that could survive over an extended period.[11]

The final three clandestine airborne operations in 1953 were also unsuccessful. The success of the BOXER operations undoubtedly raised hopes by the planners that more operations had a chance of success.

Code name HURRICANE consisted of five partisans who were to establish an operational base in the mountainous terrain southeast of Anju. This team was trained in radio communications and would maintain a constant stream of reports to its headquarters as well as setup the base. On the night of 30/31 March the team was dropped. The team landed successfully and reported in right after landing. However, two days later the team requested a helicopter rescue because enemy forces had located it. The helicopter request was not approved apparently in consideration of a potential overfight of the Chinese border and its resulting complication. The team lost contact after April 5, 1953.[12]

The RABBIT missions also had sabotage as their objectives to damage rail lines.

RABBIT I consisted of 40 partisans divided into two, twenty partisans per group. One group jumped onto a DZ about thirty miles west of Hungnam, near the village of Kwanp'Yong-Ni The second section jumped near Sogo-Ri, about fifty miles east by northeast of Pyongyang. The targets of these two sections were the rail lines running from Wonson in the east to Pyongyang in the west and the rail line from Hungnam on the east to Pyongyang on the west. Unfortunately, neither of these partisans made contact with its headquarters, therefore, RABBIT I was another failure.[13]

RABBIT II another partisan sabotage operation was dropped on the night of 7/8 April 1953. It appears the DZ selected had been used by a MUSTANG operation in September 1951. The DZ was located near the village of Kangdong. Again, the partisans disappeared without a trace![14]

The selected clandestine airborne operations coupled with the foregoing review provides the reader with comprehensive coverage of these unusual clandestine airborne operations- The primary focus being on the partisan efforts to establish a secure operational base deep in enemy controlled territory. One must consider the conditions, the combat environment, and the pressure of UN Commanders to successfully pursue the war. In those times with US personnel rotating home and an unquieting desire to conduct such operations, failures did happen.

The two primary areas of interest to the partisan mission planners were interdiction of MSRs and rail lines. However, the airforce applied greater force towards this effort with limited success. Since the Communist organization quickly mobilized manpower to begin repairs at such infrastructure air strikes, the potential impact of the partisan effort paled in comparison. The second emphasis was placed on establishing operational bases behind enemy lines. In almost all cases, except for a few days initially after the drop, the partisan bases were compromised.

No doubt some success was achieved as pointed out on SPITFIRE when Sgt. Miles observed and brought in air strikes thereby destroying a CCF Division. One could accept that success as full payment for the demise, of the SPITFIRE operation. However, such success in reality could have been an intelligence collection mission that did not require much exposure, outside the secure base area and with a much smaller team.

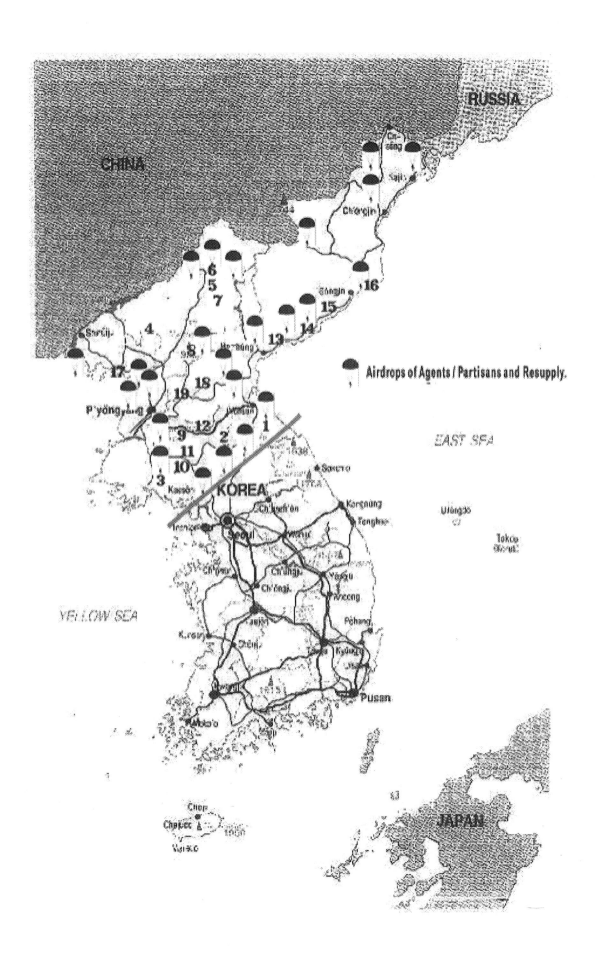

Airdrops of Agents / Partisans and Resupply.

Point	Code Name	Date	Number of Men	Number of Teams	Mission
1	Virgnia 1	15-Mar-51	24	1	Sabotage of rail and highway traffic.
2	Spitfire	18-Jun-51	16	1	Establish a guerrilla base.
3	Mustang III	22-Jan-52	19	1	Sabotage of rail traffic.
4	Mustang IV	16-Mar-52	16	1	Sabotage of rail traffic.
5	Mustang V	14-May-52	20	2	Sabotage of rail and highway traffic.
6	Mustang VI				
7	Mustang VII	31-Oct-52	5	1	Sabotage of rail and highway traffic.
8	Mustang VIII	31-Oct-52	6	1	Sabotage of rail and highway traffic.
9	Jesse James I	30-Dec-52	10	3	
10	Jesse James II	28-Dec-52	10	-	Sabotage of rail and highway traffic.
11	Jesse James III	28-Dec-52	10	-	
12	Green Dragon	25-Jan-53	97*	1	Establish a guerrilla base from which to stage interior operations.
13	Boxer I	07-Feb-53	12	4	
14	Boxer II	07-Feb-53	12	-	Sabotage of rail traffic on east coast
15	Boxer III	09-Feb-53	12	-	in conjunction with TF 95.2.
16	Boxer IV	11-Feb-53	12	-	
17	Hurricane	31-Mar-53	5	1	Establish a guerrilla base.
18	Rabbit I	01-Apr-53	40	23	Sabotage of rail traffic.
19	Rabbit II	06-Apr-53	6	-	Sabotage of rail traffic
		Total	**389**	**40**	

Between late April and 19 May 1953, 56 or 57 more partisans were sent in on this operation.

Author, LT Dillard, fitting parachute on COL Alexander, CO, FECLD for first parachute jump on to the Han River sandbar, Aug 52.

COL Lee, Korean Liaison Officer, assisted by AVIARY Korean instructors before his first parachute jump on to the Han River sandbar, Aug 52.

Author, LT Dillard, briefing COL Alexander and LTC Vanderpool on their first parachute jump on to the Han River sandbar, Aug 52. Officer on the left was the Medical Liaison Officer to FECLD.

COL Alexander, CO, FECLD (K), stands in the door with Author, LT Dillard, Jumpmaster for the Han River sandbar drop, Aug 52.

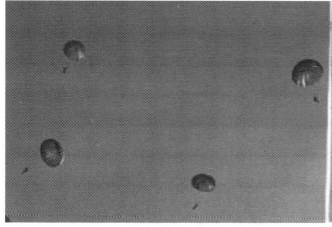

COL Lee, Korean Liaison Officer; COL Alexander, CO, FECLD; and LTC Vanderpool, Chief, Guerilla Division, FECLD made one parachute jump on the Han River sandbar.

SGT Mast assisting COL Lee, Korean Liaison Officer to FECLD (K), after jump on to the Han River sandbar, Jul 52.

LTC Vanderpool, Chief, Guerilla Division; COL Lee, Korean Liaison Officer and COL Alexander, CO, FECLD, after completing their first jump, Jul 52.

Author, LT Dillard; SGT Herbert; LT Albritton; and SGT Romano – AVIARY Jumpmasters, Seoul, Korea.

SGT Vic Romano, Senior Jumpmaster with AVIARY, conducting training jumps with the Korean Partisans from Leopard Base, Jul 52. Drop zone is the Han River sandbar, South Korea.

South Korean Minister of Defense awarding the WANRANG Medal w / SS to TLO LT Dillard, 8240 AU, Seoul, Korea, Jul 52. LT Rex Watson is next to LT Dillard and the SGT of the Field Staff.

CPT Bob Ford, USAF, stands by his C-47, which he flew on many clandestine missions in 1952. Photographed at K-16, South Korea, Jul 52.

LTG Barcas, CG, Fifth USAF presents the DFC to the Author, LT Dillard. Photographed at Fifth USAF HQ, Seoul, Korea, Aug 52.

CHAPTER VIII

PERSONAL HISTORIES - AVIARY AND OTHERS

CAPTAIN RICHARD A. ARMELLINO, US AIRFORCE:[1]

Captain Armellino had flown many clandestine airborne missions for Lt. Albritton and the other AVIARY jumpmasters as well as me at various times. Armellino was recalled to active duty for Korean service and prior to deploying to the Far East, had flown the C-46 aircraft and participated in airborne training exercises at Fort Benning, Georgia with the Ranger Training Center. Recall the Ranger Infantry Companies (Airborne) were activated and trained at Fort Benning. Major General, then Major Singlaub, was directing the training before he deployed to Korea. With this limited exposure to small unit drops on small drop zones at night, he was exposed at least to the type of classified missions he would fly in Korea.

In April 1951, Armellino was in Japan where he flew a variety of support type missions transporting troops, hauling cargo throughout Japan, and occasional trips to Korea. In early May, the Squadron Commander asked for volunteers to fly classified missions in Korea. Captain Armellino realized he could accumulate points for rotation faster, since each mission earned a point. Incidentally during the two months in Korea he accumulated 200 points for those missions and was the only volunteer from his squadron! May 13th found Armellino flying to assorted islands, making drops, landings, and unloading cargo and personnel. The two beaches he recalled were at Pyongyang-Do, and Cho-Do. He considered the beach at Cho-Do as challenging, but Pyongyang-Do straightforward. Actually landing at Cho-Do must be done when the tide is out and the landing or take-off is not exactly straightforward but at a slight angle as the beach curves a bit.

During the period of two months, Armellino indicates he had two or three co-pilots and navigators assigned temporarily to his aircraft. On one occasion while awaiting take-off instructions, Armellino said to his co-pilot, "My eyes are tearing", how come?" The co-pilot replied, "Our load of Koreans just finished lunch and ate Kimchi" Armellino had just been introduced that odious, garlic, fermented cabbage, Korean delight.

On the operational side, Armellino describes the fact that during the night prebriefings he was not provided weather updates for North Korea, some nights were fine, others not good at all. For example, he says, "On a flight towards the end of May we flew into hail and lightening for about an hour or more - St.Elmo's fire, a real violent thunderstorm." He finally broke into the clear and saw bright moonlight, flying just below the Yalu River. Realizing his position so far north, he immediately changed course and headed south. Although the flight did not encounter any antiaircraft or small arms fire, some magnesium flares came up from the ground. The navigator thought they came from Manchuria.

Armellino flew the night missions with either Lt. Albritton or me as jumpmaster. He describes his view of these two officers as follows; "These were obviously well trained and professional soldiers. They showed extreme concern for our jumpers. Their strategies are indelible in my mind even after almost 50 years. One great idea was to always fly well north of our target area so that we would be on a southerly heading into the target area to avoid listening devices and radar as much as possible. The Chinese would not expect flights well north of the combat zones."

"Another strategy was to drop from under 800 to 1000 feet in the mountains so that the hang time was a little as possible. Also drop heading across the valleys and limit fire from the MSR'S. They pursued another strategy pursued that was to locate the DZ, proceed 10-20 miles past, then circle a few times and proceed to the target and make the drop. After all of this we would place .30 caliber machine guns against the doorframes and fire at anything or nothing. All of this was done to protect our dropped troopers the best way we could. The coup de grace were fake bombs in the form of two GI gas cans dropped with a phosphorus grenades attached. They looked like a small A-bomb at 3AM on a dark night."

"As I look back on these urgent missions it is amazing how these two jumpmasters stayed alive, all those years. I recall another mission with these two guys along one clear night flying up the east coast when a radar station called and asked who we were. I had already given an estimated time of return to the Hamhung area. The radar operator suggested I not change direction, altitude, or air speed for a while. It seems a bogey, night fighter, was about 6-8 miles back and gaining on us, but a Grumman F-8 was gaining on him. I advised the jumpmasters on this situation and they leaned out from the open door and saw the bogey blow up. The mission continued."

"Another incident occurred one evening as we proceeded toward our target area. This was a radio contact mission since we were monitoring 121.5 emergency channel. An American sounding voice came on and stated he was a downed airman, but he identified himself as Peter Willy (POW). I immediately assumed he was under control by the Communists. We circled around a few times and communicated via radio to try and establish his bona fides. He gave us his wife's maiden name, college fraternity, etc. as we continued to ask him questions regarding his personalia. He asked for a helicopter for the next day. We advised we would pass the information immediately. Fifth Airforce followed up by dispatching a B-26 to the area, but the setup was suspect and nothing developed. The Fifth Airforce officer to whom I initially reported the information received a POW report listing the pilot, who had died of natural causes."

"Flying the night missions were quite interesting. Getting to the right target area and being at the proper altitude for a drop was quite a challenge. I preferred a dark, moonless night; just cannot remember if we had a full moon on any of them. I believe we flew about 8-10 missions that were radio air to ground. Also we resupplied bags of food and rice to previous groups. Some of the drops included carrier pigeons, radios, all types of grenades, and other explosives. Also dropped were collapsible bicycles."

Flying in the mountains on a dark moonless night required some different techniques. We would use one-piece 3 dimensional plastic maps. I guess about 30 inches square-2 inches high. The sectors were lettered for ease in reading coordinates. By flying at 180 miles per hour, I could follow a string knotted every inch. We held the string across the map with scotch tape. One night flying trick was to let down below the mountaintops while over the east coast ocean or a large lake. That would silhouette the mountains even on a dark night. There was a large lake in North Korea that I used quite often for that purpose. We had to be careful and not fly down along the MSRS.

The jumpmasters were very good at noticing headlights, which quite often blinked off at the sound of our plane. We also flew with engines out of sync. Someone told me that it helped confuse listening devices or maybe radar. Whenever it was possible we flew behind a mountain peak to avoid radar.

"Finally, and amazingly these missions at first were almost annoying to me; just a way to get home sooner but as I became more closely involved, it actually occurred to me that they were important. I 'd never heard of partisans or how connected we were. Very recently I read 3 or 4 books on the Korean War and in the year 2000 I finally learned the truth about North Korean anti-Communists, it is a very sobering enlightenment."

Author's Comment: Captain Armellino had some experience with troop carrier aircraft and small unit night airdrops at Fort Benning Ga. I felt comfortable flying with Armellino from the very first mission flown by him. A mutual respect quickly developed between jumpmasters who flew with Armellino that insured every mission flown was a maximized effort to succeed. With the frequent rotation of pilots and navigators, the other missions flown were quite often near misses.

STAFF LIEUTENANT GRAHAM SWANSON, ROYAL NAVY[2]

I received a letter from Lt. Swanson after he had read about activities to locate and reunite US veterans of the 8240th Army Unit which AVIARY was assigned so he wrote a few comments about his experiences with the partisans and the Escape and Evasion System that rescued him.

Swanson was assigned to the 804 FAA squadron operating from His Majesty's Ship (H.M.S.) Glory off the west coast of North Korea. Swanson also mentioned his unscheduled visits to Cho-Do and why. On April 7, 1952 Swanson's Sea Fury fighter/bomber aircraft malfunctioned when the supercharger broke up at 30,000 feet and he had to make an emergency landing in the water just off the beach at Pyongyang-Do. He says only minutes later the E&E helicopter plucked him from the water and took him to the base on the island. As a gesture of goodwill, Swanson donated his .38 caliber revolver to the rescuers.

The next incident occurred only 21 days later, when he was returning from a bombing and strafing mission of a railroad bridge at Sariwon. His aircraft engine failed again and he managed to make it to the coast. He ditched into the water just off Cho-Do, one of the partisan bases. The E&E helicopter, in the process of wincing him up had fouled the hoist cable, so he was left dangling beneath the helicopter for about three miles before reaching the island. He was promptly dropped into a rice paddy. In the process of strapping himself in he found the Mae West to be too bulky so he removed it. After that three-mile flight over the water he continually thought...about that Mae West! Even though it was April, there was still ice on the water so he arrived on the island quite numb and stiff. The boys there helped by sharing their Rye whiskey to help him warm up. Due to his situation the helicopter had to accelerate in level flight towing him like a water skier. Of course, these guys asked, "Where is your .38 revolver?" He told them, It was a Sten Gun this time and it was out there with my Mae West." " They soon returned with it." It is assumed the Mae West was still afloat near the dinghy and the Sten Gun was

57

retrieved from the dinghy.

The next time Swanson dropped in was after changing to the 802 squadron and to H.M.S. Ocean. On 4 June 1952, Swanson, while dive bombing a coastal gun position, his Sea Fury was hit by antiaircraft fire and set afire. After passing over the coastline, Swanson bailed out over the water but not far from Sokto. He had just climbed into his dinghy when he heard machine gun fire, so he jumped in the water. He then saw an American Corsair strafing the enemy positions as protection for him. Not long after this, the E&E helicopter arrived. The first thing the rescuers said upon seeing him was "Not you again!" Swanson was badly burned this time and had to be medically evacuated immediately to a hospital in Japan. He recovered and returned to England.

Swanson's final comment in his letter was "I would love to hear from any of your unit who can remember that Limey they were always picking up. My belated thanks to them all!"

Essentially, the helicopter crews that operated from the partisan base on Cho-Do, the Leopard partisan's base conducted the rescues of Lt. Swanson. The mutual support of the rescue units coupled with the partisan's knowledge of the areas provided for an excellent coordinated operation. For example, the partisans led by US advisors returned to the northwestern coastal area to reestablish partisan bases on the island. The year before, the Chinese in response to the partisan attacks along the coast, decided to push them off the islands, thereby negating any further partisan operations in that area.

RESCUE OF COLONEL SCHINTZ, USAF

Led by Captain Robert Kesslinger and Lt. James Mapp, a partisan unit DONKEY 15 sailed back into the area in mid May. They reoccupied the island of Umu-Do from where they began conducting raids along the coast. On June 7, 1952, Lt. Mapp who was operating in the vicinity of the island of Taehwa-Do, (formerly the partisan base where Lt. Adams-Acton was captured in 1951), observed an F51 shootdown near that island. He and the partisans responded to rescue the pilot. Lt. Mapp had to wait until darkness before approaching the island because it was not known whether the island was still occupied by Chinese forces. After dark, the group landed and found the island unoccupied. Soon one of the partisan squads discovered Col. Albert W. Schintz, Deputy Commander, 51st Fighter/Intercept Wing. The partisan squad leader, Mr. Sup, is a now an American citizen and resides in the Los Angles area. Col. Schintz had been on the island for 37 days after being shotdown. The Colonel bailed out over the Yellow Sea and after safely landing, secured his dinghy and paddled to the nearest island, Taehwa-Do. The F-51 pilot that Mapp had observed was not found. Schintz was evacuated and the partisans recovered their old base on Taehwa-Do. This example of the partisan rescues complimented the other capability of the US helicopters, all of which were part of an organized Evasion and Escape Program.[3]

Author's Comment: DONKEY-15 and their exploits on these northwestern islands are truly examples of courage. Again, as partisan attacks on the coastal areas began to annoy the Chinese, they, in turn, attacked and occupied the same island bases as in 1951. DONKEY- 15 once again fled, 10 miles to the south to the very small island of Nap-Som. Incidentally, the beginning of this book describes my emergency resupply mission to

DONKEY-15 to aid the partisans in moving to the safehaven partisan base on Cho-Do.

AVIARY PERSONNEL AND THEIR STORIES:

FIRST LIEUTENANT EMORY ALBRITTON[4] and I traveled together from assignments in the 82d Airborne Division to Korea. After being picked out of the personnel pipeline at Camp Drake, Japan, we were assigned to the 8240th Army Unit, also known as the Far East Command Liaison Detachment, Seoul. Korea. Initially, due to officer shortages in the unit, Albritton was made the S-4 or Logistics officer for the Command, again with the promise he would join AVIARY as soon as possible.

Although there were standing operating procedures in effect, the policy of "need to know" was not followed very well. In Albritton's case, (analogous to the earlier comment about Captain Hern and his knowledge of operations), having been the S-4 and also having visited all of the major partisan bases, the TLO organization and being thoroughly familiar with the command's logistics, he certainly could have greatly compromised the organization if he had been captured on an AVIARY mission and tortured into revealing these secrets.

Albritton joined AVIARY in early March 1952. Albritton's first mission was on March 16 that consisted of a drop of agents northeast of Pyongyang. The agents were dressed in North Korean uniforms and carried Communist made weapons. The drop was successful with no problems encountered. In May, Albritton made a partisan drop of 36 men that again was in an area northeast of Pyongyang and had no difficulty in finding the DZ. to make the drop. In between C-47/46 missions, Albritton made several B26 missions with assistants such as Sgt. Kent, Romano and Garvey. Quite often, the number of missions on the same night required several jumpmasters, and when this occurred the senior enlisted jumpmaster would execute the mission.

Albritton recalls that many of the agents carried homing pigeons in cages, strapped to their harness. Albritton had flown missions with Captain Van Fleet, the son of General Van Fleet, the Eighth Army Commander. Unfortunately, while on a normal B-26, bombing mission, Captain Van Fleet disappeared with no trace. The 8240th Army Unit, upon receiving the information scrambled to drop agents into the area. Since I was on a mission, Lt. Albritton responded immediately and dropped three agents into the suspected area where the B-26 had gone down. This drop was done before dawn of the same night he was lost. Although the quick response was remarkable, the location or facts of his loss was never discovered.

There were two B-26 pilots with whom AVIARY personnel executed many missions. The principal ones were Captain Van Fleet and Capt. Black. They worked extremely well with the AVIARY personnel and went out of their way to understand the techniques of delivery that had to be used for a successful drop from the bomb bay. The AVIARY personnel were extremely upset over the loss of Captain Van Fleet. And as indicated the guerrilla and intelligence sections of the 8240th Army Unit exploited every source to try and learn the facts of Van Fleet's disappearance.

One of Albritton's more unique experiences was a three agent team dropped with collapsible bicycles. This drop was made on a DZ. located in the northeast corner of North Korea very near the Soviet border. Although Albritton had fractured his hand while practicing the drop on the Han River sandbar, he accomplished the mission in North Korea without a problem. Albritton also was an innovator of the exploding gas drums that Captain Armellino referred to above. Albritton and Sgt. Vince Romano developed a safe way to rig the gas drums and fit them with primer cord and/or phosphorus grenades causing the gas to ignite and resemble an exploding small atomic device. Albritton was always initiating something that tested the pilot's patience, but in the end they trusted him.

On one trip to Japan to replenish AVIARY's supply of parachutes and other types of airborne gear, Albritton talked the Quartermaster out of about everything they had in the warehouse. The Japanese laborers kept loading the C-46 until the pilot asked if the aircraft might be overloaded. Of course, Albritton would never admit that so the plane took its position for take off. As the aircraft flew off the runway it barely cleared the end of the field that joined the water's edge. A small Japanese fishing boat was nearly blown over from the prop wash. The pilot summoned Albritton and me to say he would need to fly a considerable distance over water before he could finally attain the prescribed altitude to return to K-16. He said a few other unkind words and then, "I guess if you are in this kind of business you must be a little crazy." The pilot continued flying that heavy load back to K-16. Subsequently, this incident became a war story for the pilot.

Emory Albritton is one of the very few paratroopers who served on jump status throughout his military career. During his active duty from November 1942 to August 1965, Albritton made 335 static line jumps and 500 Free fall jumps, a total of 835 jumps, a remarkable airborne career by a great soldier and patriot.

In September 1952, due to a family emergency, Albritton returned to the United States on reassignment to the 77th Special Forces Group, three months ahead of normal rotation. During his assignment as the assistant leader of AVIARY, Albritton performed outstandingly, had the respect of the enlisted jumpmasters in AVIARY and commanded the respect of the 8240th Army Unit staff as well as all the different pilots and navigators with whom he worked. As head of the AVIARY team in 1952, I never doubted the professionalism and "CAN DO" attitude demonstrated by Albritton. He was " the man for all seasons" to AVIARY.

DISTINGUISHED FLYING CROSS
AWARDED TO

1ST LIEUTENANT EMORY C. ALBRITTON

1st. Lt. Emory C. Albritton, 0993286, Infantry, United States Army, is awarded the Distinguished Flying Cross. Lt. Albritton distinguished himself by extraordinary achievement while participating as Senior Jumpmaster in aerial flight over hostile territory during a nighttime highly classified mission of critical importance to the United Nations Forces engaged in ground combat in Korea. Lieutenant Albritton a member of the 8240th Army Unit, AVIARY Team without regard for his personal safety greatly aided the pilot in locating the drop zone for the successful completion of the mission. Lt. Albritton reflects great credit upon himself, the United States Army and the United States Air Force.

SGT. ORLANDO W. CHADA[5] arrived in Korea as a Ranger assigned to the Fourth Ranger Infantry Company (Airborne). He was awarded the Purple Heart and Bronze Star with V device for combat actions with the Rangers. He joined the AVIARY team in 1951 after the Ranger Companies were deactivated. He remained with the AVIARY through 1953 at the time hostilities ceased. Chade recalls flying the B-26 missions, one in particular near the Soviet border. The thought of operating near the border with Russia concerned everyone who had to do it, but the knowledge that the B-26 was fast, very maneuverable and the pilot extremely good helped offset the concern. Although the cramped space and with no visibility from the bomb bay position, until the doors were opened was not enjoyable at all.

Chada describes another mission where he was to make a drop of five agents with weather recording instruments. There were other teams for this same type of mission that I also dropped in another area in North Korea. Meanwhile, Chada using a C-47 aircraft started the approach to the DZ. and began receiving ground fire, muzzle flashes could be observed from the aircraft. Chada advised the pilot to divert to the alternate DZ. The drop was made successfully and the aircraft returned to K-16. Before clearing the aircraft as the jumpmaster climbed onto the tarmac they immediately smelled the odor of fuel. The alarm was given to not light up any cigarettes because of leaking fuel. Upon completing the physical inspection of the aircraft, numerous bullet holes were found in the fuselage and the wing tanks were leaking fuel. Fortunately, the aircraft made an almost 200 mile flight back to K-16 with leaking wing tanks and landed safely.

Finally, Chada comments on another of his B-26 missions. The operational mission went very well, no problem locating the DZ. and the drop itself was with out incident. The B-26 headed back to K-16. The pilot was advised by his flight engineer that the gear was down and safely in position. However, as they landed, the plane slammed into the runway on its belly and tore up a stretch of runway. No one was injured but that was one less B-26 available for operations.

For the mission Chada conducted near the northeast borders of North Korea and Russia he was awarded the Distinguished Flying Cross by the US Fifth Airforce Commanding General at K-16 Airforce base, Seoul, Korea. In addition to the award of the DFC, Chada also received eight awards of the Air Medal for his participation in 120 aerial flights over hostile, enemy territory in connection with clandestine airborne operations.

DISTINGUISHED FLYING CROSS
IS AWARDED TO

SERGEANT ORLANDO W. CHADA

The Distinguished Flying Cross is awarded to Sergeant Orlando W. Chada for distinguishing himself during covert operations at the Yellow Sea, between North Korea and China. Sergeant Chada completed his mission, while receiving heavy enemy fire, against his aircraft.

Author's Comment: Sgt. Chada was but another contribution the Rangers made to this classified effort. This single group of combat infantry, experienced veterans constituted a cadre of outstanding soldiers. The Rangers motto. "Rangers Lead the Way," was certainly appropriate for the Rangers of the Korean War.

SERGEANT RALPH PALMER⁶describes a different experience he had. His mission was to fly in a SA-16, an amphibious aircraft on a mission near the Russian Port City of Vladivostok, Siberia. The aircraft landed in the waters just off the port city but within range to observe several Russian ships anchored nearby. The flight took off from K-16 on June 22, 1953. Palmer describes the take off as normal, except the aircraft was a different "Duck", as it had seats and the door was closed making for a comfortable flight. This was much different from the cold and I emphasize cold, interiors of the C-46, C47, or the cramped nose or gunner's compartment of the B-26. We flew north out of K-16, much over water toward Vladivostok. Exact location was classified and may still be? We looked for our mission. Then because everyone, including the pilots and crew had concerns of the proximity of the Russian ships nearby, we took off with JATO (Jet Assisted Take-Off), resulting in an unusually quiet flight back to K-16. Often we drew fire from the enemy and our own troops as we crossed the DMZ (Demilitarized Zone). I flew several additional missions using this amphibious type aircraft where we had again to use the JATO."

For the mission enumerated above, Sgt. Palmer was awarded the Distinguished Flying Cross. Additionally, Palmer received the equivalent of 5 air medals for the 97 missions he participated in while with AVIARY.

DISTINGUISHED FLYING CROSS
AWARDED TO

SERGEANT FIRST CLASS RALPH PALMER

SERGEANT FIRST CLASS RALPH K. PALMER distinguished himself by extraordinary achievement while participating in aerial flight as a jumpmaster attached to the 6167th Operations Squadron, Far East Air Forces, on June 22, 1953. On that date, Sergeant Palmer flew on a SA-16 type aircraft on a classified night mission of great importance to the United Nations effort in Korea. After penetrating deep into enemy territory, the aircraft was subjected to heavy automatic weapons and antiaircraft fire. However, Sergeant Palmer's fast and positive identification of the target despite adverse weather conditions and enemy opposition enabled the crew to complete the operation with minimum risk to the crew and aircraft. Demonstrating high personal courage and realizing the importance of the mission, Sergeant Palmer performed his duties on the aircraft in a professional manner, directly assisting the crew in the successful completion of the mission. Through his outstanding airmanship and unselfish devotion to duty, Sergeant Palmer reflected great credit upon himself, the Far East Air Forces and the United States Army.

Sgt. Palmer was an outstanding member of the AVIARY team. He executed many of the clandestine missions as jumpmaster with great success. He was subsequently selected to be a member of the U. S. Army "Golden Knights", the premier military service parachute exhibition team that is renowned worldwide. Palmer completed a full military career and is now retired in Richmond, Virginia.

LIEUTENANT DOUGLAS C. DILLARD[7] head of the AVIARY team beginning in February 1952, I was immediately challenged with the task at hand. With the knowledge of most of the failures, already recorded, in conducting the clandestine airborne effort, I wanted to become familiar with the present staff of jumpmasters and review procedures being followed by the AVIARY staff, including security measures on the missions. Additionally, I made an effort to ensure that close coordination with the supporting airforce team was done on each mission and that a healthy respect for the jumpmasters' professional ability received a priority effort. If AVARY was to provide advice to the pilots and navigators on these pinpoint drops, the AVIARY jumpmasters must earn this respect. My airborne experience is well covered in the personnel selection section; therefore, the following is my personal description of a mission on which I was awarded the Distinguished Flying Cross.

The mission in question was conducted on May 11, 1952 using a C-46 type aircraft. The mission five-man agents drop with radio equipment, at approximately 0130 hours. The weather was fairly good, however the target location on the northwestern quadrant of North Korea near Chinnamp'O, was a challenge because of the locations of antiaircraft gun positions that would be encountered on the approaches to the drop zone. The drop zone was in a small valley that did provide defilade for the aircraft and some protection from the gun positions. What is almost never known just before a drop, is whether the gun positions have been moved nearer to your DZ. I was also awarded seven Air Medals for aerial flights over hostile enemy territory, generally in unarmed, unescorted aircraft, where deep penetrations of enemy air space was required. The total missions accumulated was 103. Fortunately, in all those missions, with the aircraft having been hit by many rounds of both automatic fire and rifle fire, I was not wounded.

DISTINGUISHED FLYING CROSS
AWARDED TO

FIRST LIEUTENANT DOUGLAS C. DILLARD

On May 11, 1952, FIRST LIEUTENANT DOUGLAS C. DILLARD, displayed extraordinary skill, devotion to duty and inspirational leadership while participating in aerial flight over enemy territory. He acted as observer and jumpmaster on a night flight, over 200 miles behind enemy lines in an unarmed cargo type C-46 aircraft. The target was located in an area where many known antiaircraft gun positions were placed. The success of the mission depended upon the jumpmaster pin -pointing the target and dropping the paratroopers on the drop zone. As the aircraft began its letdown into the target area, it was subjected to

heavy antiaircraft fire and was hit several times by flak, inflicting heavy damage to the aircraft. At this time the paratroopers became excited and tried to jump from the aircraft. Lieutenant Dillard placed himself in the open jump door and held the paratroopers from jumping. At the same time he gave instructions to the pilot which greatly aided him his evasive action as well as locating the proper DZ. Lieutenant Dillard remained calm during this action and finally jumped the paratroopers on the pin pointed DZ. The successful completion of this mission was a direct result of Lieutenant Dillard's knowledge of the terrain and his instructions to the pilot. Lieutenant Dillard's devotion to duty, and professional skill is in keeping with the highest traditions of the United States Army and the United States Airforce.

Major General Guy S. Meloy presenting Distinguished Flying Cross
to 1LT Emory C. Albritton - 12 December 1952, Fort Benning, Georgia.

Author, 1LT Dillard, INF, was presented the Distinguished Flying Cross for combat action over North Korea. Presented by LTG Barcas, Fifth Air Force Commander, Aug 52.

CHAPTER IX

RECAPITULATION
UNITED STATES AIRFORCE SPECIAL OPERATIONS, KOREA

The following recapitulation of US Airforce Special Operations during the Korean war has been extracted from the original US Airforce Special Operations Korean War Chronology prepared by Major Forrest L. Marion, USAFR, HQ. Air Force Special Operations Command/History Office, Maxwell Airforce Base, Alabama. The chronology was developed from reviews of US Airforce Organizational Records and Histories of airforce units that engaged in combat activities during the Korean War.[1]

I felt it necessary to publish this recapitulation of classified US Airforce operations during the Korean War because the record is not entirely clear as to the many missions that were flown and for whom these missions supported. Many official entities conducted clandestine airborne operations, however, only the US Airforce provided the aircraft to conduct them. In some instances a single mission may have been in support of another activity or during the mission another activity was also supported. I have attempted to at least provide a recapitulation of the officially recorded clandestine airborne missions and have totaled such at the end of each successive year of operation:[2]

1950

1-31 August.	21st Troop Carrier Squadron operated an average of thirty-three C-47 aircraft during the month conducting airdrops of personnel, equipment and supplies.
23 September	Flight A, 3d Air Rescue Squadron, with SB-17 aircraft conducted one Top Secret mission at the direction of the Far East Airforces.
24 September	Flight A, 3d Air Rescue Squadron, conducted one Top Secret mission at the direction of the Far East Air Forces.

Note: The August missions do not indicate the number that were clandestine agent/partisan drops, although the early activities of intelligence (KLO) operations were conducted as reference in BG Aderholts recollection of missions he executed in support of Colonel Brewer's operations. The September missions were apparently single acts of one or more persons.[3]

1951

1-31 January.	Aircraft, possibly SA-16s of Flight C, 2d Air Re Squadron. operating from Misawa AB, Japan, performed "some cover missions of a Top Secret Nature."

29 January	"Support Unit 4 (hereafter Unit 4), 21st Troop Carrier Squadron conducted a radio intercept mission near Yonan-Chinnampo.
31 January	Unit 4 drops one UN agent near Yonan.
1 February	Unit 4 drops five UN personnel near Chorwon-Ip'ori
13 February	Unit 4 conducts a radio intercept near Hamhung.
21 February	Unit 4/SAM conducts one radio intercept and one resupply drop at XC 6553.
22 February	Unit 4/SAM conducts two supply drops near Tokchok-Chinnampo and two radio intercepts and two personnel drops near Yonan-Chinnamp'O
23 March	In response to a US Navy request Flight D, 3d Air Rescue Squadron using an SA16 aircraft drops an eight-man life raft alongside the Saint Paul in Wonsan Bay, North Korea for a special mission.
1-30 April	Unit 4/SAM conducts 84 leaflet drops, 48 voice broadcasts and radio intercepts, 7 personnel drops and 7 resupply missions.
1-31 May	Unit 4/SAM conducts 77 leaflet drops, 21 voice broadcasts, 3 radio intercepts, 12 personnel drops and 4 resupply drops.
8 May	Flight D, 3d Air Rescue Squadron provides one SA16 and one SA17 for a Special Mission in support of the Joint Operations Center, Korea.
1 June	Fifteen agents of the Korean Air Force Special Activities Unit at Taegu parachute into North Korea to conduct sabotage activities and retrieve parts from a crashed MiG-15.
1-30 June	Unit 4/SAM conducts 66 leaflet drops, 25 broadcasts, 3 radio intercepts, 18 personnel drops and 1 resupply drop.
	Major John J. Dean flew an H-5 Helicopter deep into enemy territory to pick up a UN agent, he is escorted and contact made from a Unit 4/SAM, C-47 aircraft, the first attempt was unsuccessful, second try by Lt. Donald J. Crawford is successful. Helicopter subjected to anti-aircraft fire but returned undamaged.

1-31 July	Unit 4/SAM now commanded by Captain Rex W. McDowell, conducts 36 leaflet drops, 28 voice broadcasts, 2 personnel drops and 1 resupply drop.
	Detachment 1 (formerly Detachment F) 3d Air Rescue Squadron flies a total of 13 helicopter sorties evacuating thirty-seven POWs who have escaped behind enemy lines.

1952

1 April	Baker flight of the 6167th Operations Squadron is designated to take over all combat missions.
1-30 April	Baker flight flies a total of 188 leaflet sorties, 10 voice broadcasts and 66 classified sorties. Three C-47 aircraft are damaged by enemy ground fire one enlisted man from the Psychological Warfare Section is killed in action by flak.
1-31 May	Baker flight commanded by Captain James S. Garrison, flies a total of 188 leaflet drops, 21 voice broadcasts and 69 classified sorties.
7-9 May	Flights A and C, 3d Air Rescue Squadron conduct a "highly classified mission, requiring two open seas landings, utilizing SA-16 aircraft.
19-20 May	Flight C, 3d Air Rescue Squadron conducts a highly classified mission perhaps connects to the 7-9 May mission with a senior officer aboard.
1-30 June	Baker flight flies a total of 170 leaflet drops, 19 voice broadcasts, and 81 classified sorties.
1-31 July	Baker flight flies a total of 142 leaflet drops, 13 voice broadcasts, 69 classified sorties and 79 flare sorties.
1-31 August	Baker flight flies a total of 182 leaflet sorties, 37 voice broadcasts, 79 classified sorties, and 73 flare sorties.
28 August	Flight C, 3d Air Rescue Squadron flies four separate missions in SA-16s.
1-30 September	Baker flight flies a total of 214 leaflet sorties, 29 voice broadcasts, 69 classified sorties ands 96-flare sorties.
19 September	Two SA-16s of flight A, 3d Air Rescue Squadron conduct fly classified missions.

1-31 October	Baker flight flies a total of 202 leaflet sorties, 34 voice broadcasts, 88 classified Missions.
1-30 November	Baker flight flies a total of 203 leaflet sorties, 25 broadcasts, 77 classified sorties, and 88 flare sorties.
1-31 December	Baker flight flies a total of 137 leaflet sorties, 10 voice broadcasts, 47 classified sorties and 13 flare sorties.
8 December	Baker flight B-26 bomber is seriously damaged by antiaircraft fire while conducting a classified mission near the town of Ullyu, North Korea. The aircraft and crew return safely, except the Pilot Major Lawrence E. Freligh who was severely wounded. The aircraft landing was of a miraculous nature for which the pilot was awarded the Distinguished Service Cross.

1953

I January-30 June	Baker flight conducted a total of 844 leaflet sorties, 609 classified sorties, and 298 flare sorties.
March-May period	Baker flight practices for a snatch pickup of the downed crew of a B-29. The crew is in the hands of operation GREEN DRAGON personnel with whom radio contact is established and supply drops made during this period for the crews comfort.
24 May	Baker flight attempts the snatch pickup of the downed airmen however it is a trap and the approaching aircraft comes under heavy ground fire and must abort. The aircraft was heavily damaged but there were no injuries to the aircraft crew.
1-17 July	Baker flight conducts 73 leaflet sorties, 117 classified sorties and 101 flare sorties. (Over 7,000 flares were dispensed).

Note: It is not possible to total the number of personnel engaged in these classified missions. I participated in 110 of the flights reflected for 1952. On each missions the numbers of either agents or partisans varied. As I recall there were no official recording of the number of indigenous personnel, however, the aircrews possibly estimated the number after completion of the mission.[4]

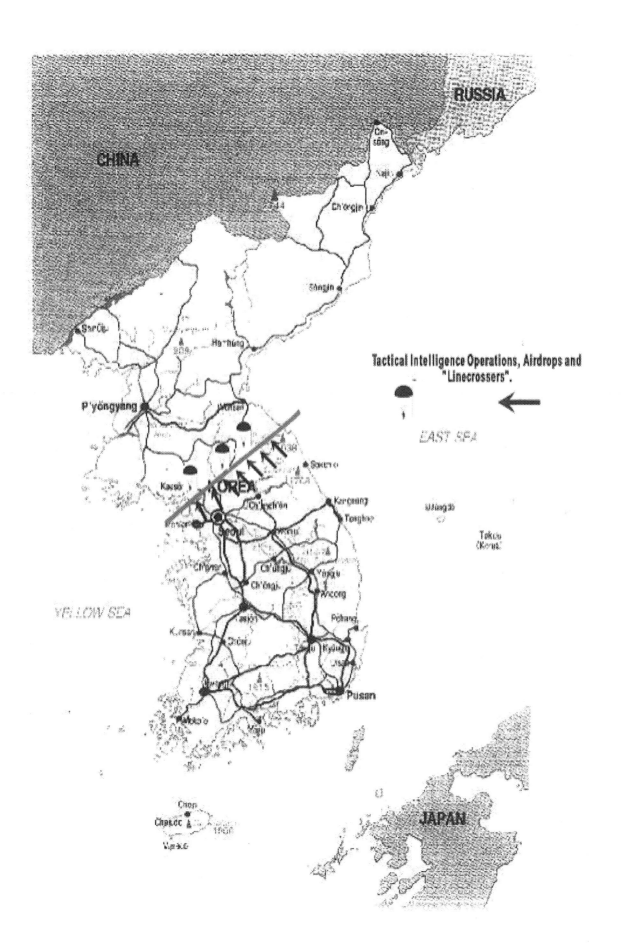

Tactical Intelligence Operations, Airdrops and "Linecrossers".

CHAPTER X

ANALYSIS OF CLANDESTINE AIRBORNE OPERATIONS

As I developed the material for this subject of clandestine airborne operations during the Korean War it seemed straightforward to simply focus on the most significant airborne operations and then succinctly review all that occurred. However, the more the I reviewed the material and discussed it with persons who had absolutely no knowledge of the activities the more I felt an obligation to analyze the data, compare it to several conditions that existed at that time in Korea and conditions that developed later. The objective of the analysis is to test the data against probable conditions that influenced the exceedingly high rate of failures in the airborne portion of the missions and the probable influencing factors that also inhibited the partisan activities on the ground.

To set the basis for the analysis I have identified the following conditions for review and analysis:

1. The Eighth Army and Far East Commanders' demands for both intelligence and partisan actions to inhibit the enemy forces.

2. The leader and staff of the Eighth Army Miscellaneous Group, BAKER Section, the Far East Command Liaison Group and AVIARY/UNPIK.

3. The US Fifth Airforce Command, Staff and Flight Squadrons.

4. North Korean Terrain and Environmental Conditions.

5. The Fluid Battlefield 1950-1951.

6. Stabilization of the Frontlines 1951-1954.

7. Soviet Integrated Air Defense System.

8. Unusual high rate of successful flights of unarmed cargo aircraft operating deep into enemy air space. (Why were none shot down?)

The foregoing conditions need to be reviewed in light of how each independently effected the outcome of the clandestine airborne operations that initially were successful but became less successful and eventually failed.

1. The Eighth Army and Far East Commanders' demands for intelligence and partisan actions to inhibit the enemy forces:

DISCUSSION. The invasion of the Republic of South Korea caught the United States off guard with no expectation of such action by the small Communist country of North Korea. By the same token, the United States Armed Forces were in no condition to actively defend South Korea much less aggressively pursue an all out war. I will try and confine my comments to a succinct review of the commander's needs. With only token US forces withdrawing southward into the Pusan perimeter, the US government began its buildup of the armed forces and deployment of such forces not only to Korea but also to reinforce its deployments in Europe to strengthen the NATO Forces.

Meanwhile General Walker, Commander, US Eighth Army confronted by the hordes of North Korean Forces had urgent demands for intelligence to find and fix the enemy, and to destroy them. To accomplish such tasks the commander must utilize every source available to him. In the case at hand, the concept of employing the North Korean anti-Communists, some already attacking enemy forces behind the lines, was no doubt seen as a multiplier of force to draw off some of the North Korean forces attacking the US Eighth Army. Since partisan elements were already operating from off-shore islands and on the peninsula, behind enemy lines, the next logical step was to develop an air delivery capability of inserting partisans and intelligence agents in areas deep inside enemy territory. There they would begin to influence the diversion of enemy frontline troops to rear area security. The foregoing considerations influenced the activation of the US Eighth Army's' Miscellaneous Group and its BAKER SECTION. In addition, in October 1950 Colonel McGee, the leader of the Miscellaneous Group, also influenced the activation of the Eighth Army Ranger Company to engage in guerrilla and counter-guerrilla operations. It subsequently became an infantry attack company with the 25th Infantry Division.[1]

At the same time, the G-2 Far East Command began its planning for such type operations. At the insistence of Major General Edward M. Almond, Chief of Staff, to the Commander in Chief, Pacific, the provisional Raider Company was organized for deployment to Korea. Personnel for this company were recruited from the General Headquarters and Special Troops in Tokyo, subsequently known as the X Corps Raiders. In addition, the General Headquarters Staff activated The Special Activities Group that consisted of American officers and some US enlisted men, but mostly Koreans. Its mission was counter-guerrilla operations, especially needed in Korea due to the large numbers of NK guerrillas and stragglers in the rear areas of the US Eighth Army. US personnel for these two units came from GHQ and Special Troops resources in Tokyo. 1st Lt. Brewer at this time had been handling the fledging AVIARY operation that essentially dispatched intelligence agents by airborne means into North Korea on short notice tactical intelligence collection missions. However, the Korean Liaison Office also dispatched agents into North Korea, usually on longer-range missions. In this instance we see a fast paced air delivery activity geared to directly support the Eighth Army Commander's intelligence requirements. These dynamic intelligence requirements could immediately impact for good or bad on the troops of the Eighth Army if successful. Remember the AVIARY operations are separate and distinct from the newly organized BAKER SECTION that was devoted to partisan operations. After reading the cases of

VIRGINIA I AND SPITFIRE OPERATIONS, one can visualize the pressure to set-up a partisan base deep into enemy territory and its potential to accomplish both intelligence collection missions and support attacks against enemy forces, sabotage of enemy infrastructure, and influence the diversion of enemy forces away from the frontlines.[3]

In the cases referred to above, the unit entities were alluded to as "elite units," and the accompanying thought that they must be manned by outstanding soldiers, the best of the lot. While the foregoing units were being formed in Korea and Japan, the Ranger Infantry Companies (Airborne) were also being formed at Fort Benning, Georgia, and again to be manned by the best of the lot. Most of the men actually came from the 82d Airborne Division.

The foregoing unit organizations were conceived within an exceedingly short period of time, and were in retrospect, conceptualized for specialized warfare in both guerrilla and counter-guerrilla operations. As the urgency of wartime conditions dictated, except for the Miscellaneous Groups partisans, the other units were diverted to line infantry duties with little if any participation in the conceived mission as an elite unit to engage in guerrilla or counter-guerrilla operations. As always, a Commander's view of his needs drive the manner in which his forces will be employed. The one additional facet of utilization of elite units is that most line unit commanders view these units as a "creaming of the unit," with soldiers that would be an outstanding asset to their more conventional force. And since the commander has the control, he will exercise the elite units to do the impossible. Such utilization results in the decimation of these units. Such was the fate of the Ranger Infantry Companies (Airborne).

An interesting facet leading to the deactivation of the Ranger Infantry Companies (Airborne) was the position taken by Brigadier General Gilman C. Mudgett, G-3, US Eighth Army. At the time the Rangers' fate was to be decided by General Ridgway Mudget, on 14 May 1951, stated "A Rangers Battalion at army level would meet with general approval." The thought was to assign a Ranger Battalion to Colonel McGee's Miscellaneous Group to conduct guerrilla operations. The author has addressed this potential earlier in this book but at the company level. General Ridgway after his review of the Eighth Army Commander's recommendations rejected them and sided with the inactivations. His position was seconded by General J. Lawton Collins, US Army Chief of Staff, who stated in DA message 95587, "One of the compelling reasons for the decision to inactivate these companies was the fact that deep patrol missions by small units for which the rangers are intended, are most difficult in the Far East Command by reason of the racial differences between the Oriental and the Caucasian". General Ridgway also addressed the language barrier in his considerations. I have addressed this cultural problem, especially the language barrier that was not overcome throughout the Korean War.[4]

The irony of General Collin's position was that during his visit to Korea in 1950 he was concerned about NK guerrillas. His answer was the activation of the Ranger Infantry Companies (Airborne), with a distinct guerrilla role behind the lines. On 29 August 1950, General Collins stated his position in a memorandum supporting the companies' activation and deployment to Korea. In a period of eleven months these "elite units" disappeared from the active army rolls. The above analysis leads one to the conclusion that too much staff action, with a limited knowledge of the conditions in Korea caused a host of unit activations with roles in the Guerrilla and Counter-Guerrilla field, but once in country, were employed in other than their intended mission.[5]

2. The Leaders and staffs of the Eighth Army Miscellaneous Group, BAKER SECTION, Far East Command Liaison Group and AVIARY/UNPIK:

BAKER SECTION

DISCUSSION: Colonel McGee as the leader of the Eighth Army's Miscellaneous Group did not have experience in conducting airborne operations, especially these more focused small unit type operations. He had to rely on subordinates who were airborne qualified, but most of the staff had no experience in unconventional warfare, except in some cases such as Captain Hern who had some experience during World War II. Seemingly, the immediate combat environment influences the conduct of these type operations. Without a more detailed analysis of the enemy Interior Security Forces capabilities the operations are easily neutralized. Often in intelligence collections operations, the enthusiasm to conduct operations for the sake of an operation overrides the prevailing security considerations. In both instances of VIRGINIA I and the SPITFIRE operations, there were serious problems one notes in reviewing their execution. In researching this story, I have yet to locate any data regarding the development of an Intelligence analysis of potential security forces and practices that existed in the denied area chosen for the two operations, notwithstanding the additional problems that occurred in their execution.[6]

I have already referred to the use of the two British Army officers, Captain Anderson and Lt. Adams-Acton, both of whom led or participated in the only operations comprised of both Caucasian and Asian elements. These selections were evidently made based on Captain Anderson's W.W.II experience with the British SAS and his strong endorsement of Lt. Adams-Acton to Colonel McGee who accepted him into the organization even though the Lieutenant had no World War II experience. As it turned out, this Lieutenant brought out the few survivors of the ill-fated SPITFIRE operation. Although there were no US officers participating in this operation there were US ranger enlisted men. The performance of these US Rangers on both operations was outstanding. The Rangers demonstrated on a smaller scale what a battalion of US Rangers could have accomplished on a greater scale.[7]

AVIARY

DISCUSSION: As commented upon earlier, the AVIARY operation began earlier in the conflict. However, its role was more oriented towards the airborne dispatch of intelligence agents, later assuming the role also for the training and dropping of partisans. The AVIARY operation was under the staff direction of the Intelligence Division of the Far East Command Liaison Detachment, 8240th Army Unit. Its commanders changed frequently so they normally did not get personally involved in day to day activities. The Staff Directors coordinated between staffs and planned the operations.

Various collection teams, oriented towards their own specialty, reviewed the intelligence requirements placed upon them from the national level down through tactical commanders. These requirements influenced the target areas where collection operations needed to be conducted. These targets influenced the selection of a clandestine airborne mission to access the target area. Once these selections were made, the indigenous agent or team was made available to AVIARY for airborne training and AVIARY personnel coordinated with the respective USAF element for drop zone selection. Airforce intelligence personnel reviewed air defense activities in the area as well as the best approaches to fly to the drop zone. Once the drop zone had been selected, the AVIARY personnel advised the collection team leader to determine its acceptability, taking into consideration the effects of either the terrain or the distance the indigenous personnel must walk to their base of operations. Once that overall coordination was completed. The mission was executed. During this process the AVIARY personnel were never told what the mission was or where it was to be conducted. The AVIARY mission was to train, drop and resupply the indigenous personnel with no involvement in the ground execution of the mission.[8]

I felt is important to explain the role of AVIARY and its limited role and knowledge of the operations. Although not having knowledge of the intelligence planning or extent of research conducted by the planning staffs, I never became aware of any extensive counter-espionage activities to protect any of the operations. The extent of the units' Intelligence staff or S-2 seemed to be confined to issuing access passes and establishing security posts to the facility. During the period I was with AVIARY, there were no security briefings or updating of known or potential espionage activities around the unit's facilities or actions that were directed against the unit's personnel or facilities. After AVIARY assumed the support mission for the partisans, the Intelligence and Guerrilla Divisions in the headquarters worked very closely, probably to the extend that the principal of "need to know" was ignored.[9]

The potential for compromise of operations even extended to the actual airdrop. On many occasions, due to aircraft scheduling, several missions were combined. For example, on February 19, 1952 when the Chinese agent blew up the C-46 aircraft with a hand grenade, the aircraft had been scheduled for more than one drop of different teams. Since none of the jumpmasters were fluent in either Korean or Chinese there is a possibility some of the agents conversed with each other and compromised their missions. Several missions were flown that way and may have compromised the missions in some way, either by revealing their objective, location or their cover. In reflecting upon these operations years later and after several years of intelligence and counter-intelligence experience, I only regret the failure to recognize the potential for compromise in conducting these repeated airborne operations at that time.

Before the assignment to Korea, I was a product of W.W.II airborne combat and peacetime duty with the 82d. During the period from the end of World War II to the beginning of the Korean War I was not exposed to more than routine physical security duties such as exterior or interior guard, nothing of note regarding security practices of the Communist controlled countries and their internal security controls.

As a general rule I believe that the average US officer and soldier had little knowledge or regard for the homeland security practices the communists had already implanted in the countries such as the Democratic Republic of North Korea. Recall the McCarthy hearings that were reprehensible in the manner in which they were conducted, did reveal an overall lack of appreciation for security practices. One in the United States Army Reserves could receive classified training documents through the US Postal

73

Service. These revelations influenced a new look at security that lead to the "need to know" concept and other needed security practices, but did not permeate the Armed Services in time to adequately prepare for the Korean War.[10]

As more information became available about the Communist security practices, the US government became proactive in developing educational security programs that influenced improved security practices through the government and the armed forces. These improvements did not come in time to influence better security practices in Korea. In Frederick W. Cleaver et al.", UN Partisan Warfare in Korea," it is pointed out that there was a needless loss of partisans and agents that continued unabated even in the face of great losses.[11]

Recall operation GREEN DRAGON, the largest in number of partisans ever involved in an operation occurred 24-25 January 1953 when 97 agents/partisans dropped near Kochang, about forty miles west of Pyongyang to establish a guerrilla base. And after a two month hiatus with no radio contact, contact was reestablished and on May 18-19 when an additional fifty-seven partisans and supplies were airdropped. In addition, the GREEN DRAGON reported they had five downed airmen so The "Snatch pickup" for the airmen was scheduled. As the aircraft approached the pickup point it was fired upon immediately so the mission was aborted. GREEN DRAGON operation was written off. The question remains, "Was there any intelligence analysis done to reestablish the bona fides of this group?"[12]

Evidently, the fervent desire to finally conduct a successful clandestine airborne operation of this magnitude overruled security considerations. The Far East Command Liaison Detachment of the 8240th Army Unit was the operations element of the US Army clandestine agent collection program and the guerrilla division of the unit that planned and directed the guerrilla activities. Lt. Col. Jay D. Vanderpool headed the guerrilla division and supervised such activities, while on the other hand LTC. Robert Doupe headed the Intelligence Division and had direct supervision of the AVIARY team. Since, I had no direct interface with the planning of these operations only their execution of the airborne portion; the extent of intelligence and security considerations that went into the planning of these operations would be mere speculation. I do, however, know from first hand experience that records were not adequately maintained or locations recorded of all the drop zones that had been used as well as the frequency and number of airborne missions conducted in the same location or its immediate vicinity. For example in 1951, the drop zone for MUSTANG II near the town of Kangdong, was used again in April 1953 by Rabbit II and the personnel were lost immediately.

One would surmise that with the stabilization of the front lines and peace talks underway, Interior Security Forces would be stronger and no doubt maintain checks of these drop zones previously used by the partisans. One could speculate that the desire to produce and execute a successful operation did override detailed intelligence analysis so no significant attention was devoted to security ramifications that perhaps would have militated against operations.[13]

3. The US Fifth Airforce Command, Staff and Flight Squadrons:

DISCUSSION: To avoid redundancy in this review of the US Airforce's role in the Clandestine Airborne Operations, it is suffice to record that as the Korean War began, as in the case of the US Army. The US Airforce was also not prepared for its forthcoming role in the unconventional warfare endeavor. There were repeated rotations of flight crews, modifications of aircraft and the failure of the US Airforce to select any of its experienced personnel from World War II who had engaged in related types of operations. Plans should have been put into place for the purpose of setting up training programs for pilots and crews that would be called upon to perform these clandestine airborne missions. Only after the debacle of VIRGINIA I with its location seemingly compromised by repeated flights over its area and the daylight drop of supplies, was the effort taken seriously by Senior Airforce personnel. Steps were taken to organize Special Mission squadrons and to begin stabilizing pilots and crews who would perform the missions[14]

Again, it is pointed out that the Airforce operations staffs who conducted the briefings and debriefings did not keep track of the drop zone location or other data. This information would have raised questions in their minds as to the potential for compromise by returning repeatedly to the same locations to drop agents or partisans. Notwithstanding, the need to resupply the indigenous personnel in the same general vicinity of their drop. Of course, it is recognized that agents would leave the area of their drop and most likely if resupplied it would be at another location, distant from the original drop zone. Generally, the briefings consisted of a review of known gun positions, watch stations along the flight route to the drop zone, and any air defenses around the drop zone. During the debriefing the intelligence staff would elicit any new sightings regarding air defenses observed during the operation. Other than these routine sessions about the actual flights there was no other discussions regarding security or personnel physical checks for personal items that could compromise the personnel if captured. There was never any discussion between the crews and the jumpmasters as to what cover story or supporting documentation that was to be used in the event of capture. On reflection, with the number of agents and partisans that had already been captured, one had to assume, a cover story would not hold up with this great potential of being identified by the agents or partisans already in custody of the North Koreans or Chinese.[15]

In the case of Captain Armellino, the C-46 pilot who flew about 200 missions while in Korea he maintains he never knew the identity of the unit for which he flew. He did know the jumpmaster by name, but nothing else about them or the agents he was dropping or their missions.   Since the crews rotated so regularly I assume their knowledge of the operations and personnel equated to that of Captain Armellino.[16]

Additionally, other operational elements in country such as the Fifth US Airforce unit and a national agency element also utilized these same aircrews and aircraft for the same type of operations. It must be assumed there was little if any cross coordination of drop zones already used or for potential use. Multiple operating elements thereby created the potential for compromise simply by making frequent drops in the vicinity or on the same drop zone. One must assume this facet of coordination should have been questioned at the time the mission was being planned and the selected drop zone selected.

4. North Korean Terrain and Environmental Conditions:

DISCUSSION: As evidenced by the locations of drop zones selected by the planners of the clandestine airborne operations, the presence of mountainous and hilly terrain no doubt influenced their selection. Of paramount importance was an unimpeded approach to the drop zone with the aircraft at altitudes that masked them from enemy radar and access to main supply routes (MSR), usually one of the targets for either observation or sabotage. When one looks at the areas of the partisan drops, particularly the larger formations, they generally fall near or on portions of the mountain chain that runs along the east coast of Korea. The mountain chain on the western side of Korea extends from just below the Yalu River south to the northwest of Pyongyang. Again this area provided the potential masking of the aircraft from radar contact as well as good bases from which the partisans could operate.[17]

The mountain areas west and north of Wonsan Harbor was used repeatedly for both agent and/or partisan drops on the east and in the vicinity of Yonan-Chinnampo on the west. In 1952, I made drops near the Yonan-Chinnampo area where the aircraft was subjected to small-arms fire and hits forcing the missions to abort.

The rivers running north to south presented potential problems to movement by the agents or partisans, especially those operating in larger groups and with more gear and weapons to carry. Exfiltration for these groups usually planned for them to move south parallel to the rivers or move east or west toward the coasts for pickup by small craft off shore.

Individual or small numbers of agents with little gear to carry often could be dropped closer to inhabited areas in less hilly or mountainous terrain. The same considerations had to be followed in selecting the approach to the drop zone as well as the potential to fly at low altitudes so a hill mass would screen the aircraft from radar contact.

Weather has already been seen as an inhibiting factor for airborne operations due to either high winds or reduced visibility for the drop. While on the ground snow and flooding of ground areas posed problems for the agents or partisans. In the case of operation VIRGINIA I it almost immediately encountered freezing temperatures and heavy snows that had a disastrous effect on the operation. In summer months, the heavy rains caused rising streams and flooding rivers to inhibit ground movement or even the recovery of supplies dropped to the waiting agents or partisans.[18]

The coastal areas where exfiltration plans often called for the operation to move to the coast for pickup were inhibited by high tides, storms and rocky coast lines that presented danger to the recovery craft as it made its way for the pickup. In spite of these problems there were successful exfiltrations.

In review of the foregoing terrain or environmental conditions that prevailed, we see they directly influenced drop zone selections as well as lines of ground exfiltration upon the completion of the operation. Since, many of these operations were lost as the saying goes "without a trace," one can only speculate on the reason for failure. Did one of these conditions contribute to the failure or did it directly cause the failure?

5. The Fluid Battlefield 1950-1951:

DISCUSSION: Any type of airborne operation is susceptible to Interior Security Forces as well as regular combat arms units. With the beginning of the Korean War in June 1950 and extending into the period of the US Eighth Army's march to the Yalu, conditions on the ground permitted the drop of hundreds of agents for tactical intelligence collection. After the entrance of the Chinese Communist Forces and the resultant withdrawal of the UN Forces south below the original 38th parallel, the fluidity of the battlefield began to change. Conducting partisan activity along the west coast of Korea, particularly, influenced the North Korean and Chinese Forces to place increased numbers of security forces along both coasts and attack several partisan island bases on the west coast. As the summer of 1951 approached, the Interior Security of North Korea had improved immensely. It is reported that over 70,000 troops were devoted to interior security which subsequently increased as the peace talks took form in July 1951[19] Additional interior security practices were developed. For example, small groups of soldiers were stopped and checked repeatedly, therefore, agent teams had to be increased in size to preclude such checks.

With a lower level of combat action on the front and fewer changes in the frontline, the interior security became more formal with registration of citizens, development of informants, and reinforced police in the rural areas.

As a result of these changes, the area of operations became more difficult in which to operate successfully. However, the clandestine airborne effort continued unabated.

6. Stabilization of the Front Lines, 1951-1954:

DISCUSSION: The foregoing section relates the factors that begin to impact on the conduct of clandestine airborne operations. The very nature of the Korean peninsula with dedicated interior security forces demonstrates the difficulties that must be overcome to successfully execute such operations. Over the period of August 1950 to the end of the War, July 1954, hundreds of clandestine airborne agent and partisan drops were made. From a numbers standpoint one could surmise that North Korea had been saturated with UN agents and partisans. After the sabotage of the C-46 aircraft in February 1952 it is alleged that groups of agents on the ground essentially ran into each other in the immediate area where the aircraft crashed. The presence of such large numbers of agents on the ground would seemingly not go unobserved by these security forces. Therefore one could also surmise that these operational personnel had been compromised earlier and as more agents were dropped in, swelling the ranks with additional compromised UN personnel.[20]

An example of the efforts to reward members of the People's Volunteer Army of Communist China for the capture of Americans and their agents were "Rules of Encouragement of Capturing the Wanted American Imperialist Agents through Rewards." Appendix C is a copy of such Rules of Encouragement that was published and posted at various traffic control points in North Korea in May 1952. Appendix D is a copy of an article that appeared on page 1 of Southern Daily in Communist China dated March 28, 1953. The headline reads: American Imperialist Airborne Agent Wang Chi captured by the People's Volunteer Army Troops. (Author's Comment: This article contains an error on the number of agents allegedly captured and alludes to their mission to monitor the effect of bacterial agents).

Assuming some validity of the claims made in the article, it is possible that the captured agents were in operation one of the BOXER drops in February 1953 or in an unlisted mission that is also quite possible. In one part of the cited article, the Chinese refer to nine agents and in another part state five agents were captured. The date captured however is different than the BOXER drops. In any event, it is interesting to read about the capture and the description of articles carried by the agents, including pigeons. For whatever reason, the Chinese may have changed the numbers of agents and the date of the drop in order not to provide any verification to the AVIARY TEAM for the losses.

The nature of the activities of the operation GREEN DRAGON would seemingly fit into this category and as the operation continued more assets were fed into the compromised operation that almost resulted in the loss of an aircraft and its crew. The failure of the GREEN DRAGON operation alone accounted for about 159 agents and partisans, not to mention the gear, codes, etc.[21]

7. Soviet Integrated Air Defense:

DISCUSSION: Although there has been considerable references made to the effective use of radar in the air war no mention is made of the effectiveness of the Soviet Integrated Air Defense System against the troop carrier, slow flying aircraft. I have detailed my exciting experience near Pyongyang in 1952 while on a mission aboard a B-26 that was detected by radar and the radar directed searchlights. Ralph Wetterhahn, a former pilot who flew 80 combat missions over North Vietnam, details his research of Russian Archives and personal interviews with former Russian senior officers of the Soviet airforce and their Korean tour. I feel it is necessary to relate some of his findings regarding the Russians of MIG Alley because they support to some extent my analysis.

Wetterhahn published his research in the August 2000 edition of the "Retired Officer Magazine." This article contributes a great deal to understanding the Soviet role in providing an Air Defense System to the North Koreans and subsequently the Chinese Communist Forces. I want to provide an insight regarding the quick development of the Soviet Air Defense Integrated system. According to Wetterhahn's interview of Soviet Colonel Yevgeniy Pepelyayev, " I thought it would end very quickly because the North Koreans were moving so rapidly, then there came (the Inchon Landing)." Everything changed as U. N. Forces surged toward the Yalu River, threatening to occupy all of Korea. The Colonel recalls, "In October (1950), Stalin decided that direct Russian involvement was necessary to prevent defeat." With this fiat from Stalin a maximized effort was made to move into the combat mode. As we know the Russians remained at bases in Manchuria from which they operated across the Yalu River and perceived safety from the US Airforce.[22]

Although the UN fighters held their own and actually maintained air superiority, except for occasional dog fights in the area known as MIG Alley, the B-29s suffered many losses due to the effectiveness of the Soviet Integrated Air Defense System. The effectiveness of the Soviet directed radar coupled with coordinated MIG flights inflicted these losses. In his article "Black Tuesday Over NAMSI," Earl McGill, a B-29 Pilot during the Korean War describes his fifteen minutes of hell. One B-29 out of 9 survived that day and returned to base with a hole in its tail section large enough for a man to crawl through.

On October 23, 1951the Bombers of the 3307th Bombardment Wing took off from Kadena, Okinawa for this mission. On that day, according to McGill that mission lost 28 killed in action and 24 wounded in action the greatest number of casualties for any single US Airforce action of the war. "The week of October 1951 signaled a revolution in the aerial war," wrote historian Walter J. Boyne in Beyond the Wild Blue. Shortly after NAMSI, according to McGill, all daylight B-29 raids were stopped switching to night raids only.[23]

I felt the foregoing description of the effectiveness of the Soviet Integrated Air Defense System directly influenced a change in US Airforce tactics. However, this change did not altogether change the impact of the air defense system. On 10 June 1952, the nighttime raids proved just as deadly. Four B-29s were caught in the Soviet searchlights over Kwaksan at the southern end of MIG alley. Twelve MIGs attacked them and three bombers went down, one made it back to Kimpo Airfield and safety. These types of encounters occurred repeatedly. The Soviet Integrated Air Defense System performed very well with its combination of radar alert, tracking of the aircraft, and radar direction of the searchlights and antiaircraft fire. These features coupled with the Soviet fighter squadrons operating from either Manchurian or Siberian sanctuaries took its toll on the B-29s.[24]

While we see these great interceptions of UN bomber flights and the resultant aerial battles, there is no reported instance of a troop carrier aircraft encountering a similar experience. Yet, clandestine airborne missions were conducted in and around MIG Alley. I made several trips into that area to locations such as Uiju, Sinuiju Kwaksan and Huichon, including flying along the south side of the Yalu River at the beginning of early morning twilight. The aircraft could not only be tracked by radar but also observed by the naked eye from the ground. In none of the cases was the aircraft fired upon, except in some cases near the drop zone as the aircraft came in on a low altitude approach to make the drop. In those instances the fire was made by either small arms or small caliber automatic weapons.

To continue a review of the Soviet radar capabilities, I found in the Wetterhahn article the answer to the complaints voiced by US Airforce pilots. The major complaint according to US Airforce Colonel Walker Mahurin was the fact that he and his pilots did not trust the Ground Control Intercept Radar Operators. All to often the US Interceptors were scrambled but found no MIGs in the area as reported by the radar operators. According to Soviet Colonel Aleksandr Orlov, who was in charge of Soviet electronic reconnaissance there, "Radio receivers were positioned on top of mountains to pick up takeoff and landing transmissions from airfields in South Korea. At Antung, my unit monitored these receivers. The Americans were doing the same, listening to our calls. So, especially when there was bad weather at our bases, we would make fake radio transmissions to lure the US planes into air where they found no opponents." Although this ploy was not recognized, Colonel Mahurin when visiting one of the radar sites learned for the first time that they were fighting the Soviet Airforce.[25]

When one takes into consideration the effectiveness of the Soviet built and manned integrated air defense system and its effect on the B-29 bombers, coupled with the radar expertise as demonstrated by Colonel Orlov, they certainly did monitor the troop carrier aircraft, but took no action to attack them, Why? Perhaps someday either Soviet Archives or still classified US Airforce archives may answer this question.[26]

8. Successful Clandestine Airborne Operations With No Loss Of Aircraft:

DISCUSSION: George Washington said in 1777 in a well-known letter discussing the problems of military intelligence, that 'upon secrecy success depends in most enterprises of the kind, and for want of it, they are generally defeated, however well planned or promising of favorable issue'. Within the British Special Operations Executive adopted the old secret-service proverb that lays down this 'three can keep a secret, if two of them are dead'. I feel it a bit convincing that while conducting of clandestine airborne operations during the Korean War, repeated instances occurred that indicated a compromise of security that were either not recognized or were ignored as US personnel rotated at end of their tour or inadequate security procedures occurred.[27]

In the chapter addressing the evolution of the clandestine airborne operations it should be recalled that as a result of the failed VIRGINIA I and SPITFIRE operations coupled with the breakup of a North Korean spy-ring in the Pusan area, BAKER SECTION operations were transferred to AVIARY. Additionally, upon the outlawing of the Communist Party (South Korean Labor Party) after the 1948 elections, its Chairman Pak Hon Yong, fled to North Korea and became a ranking cabinet member of the Kim Il Sung government. From his position in the North Korean government he directed the communist underground movement in South Korea. The principle activities of the communist underground that included guerrilla raids were located in southwest Korea. Although the magnitude of guerrilla activity was countered by a force of two S. Korean Infantry Divisions under LTG Paik Sun Yup, the extent of espionage and penetration of both South Korean governmental entities and the UN Forces is still not known. As late as April 1953 there were small guerrilla holdouts operating from the bases located in the Taibaik mountain plateau.

In reviewing the various operations that were initiated via clandestine airborne drops that ended in failure there is good reason to believe a compromise of the total concept of the clandestine operations occurred. Specifically, operations such as the partisan operation Bigboy were compromised early in its initiation on the ground. The operation continued until the debacle of the attempted rescue of the navy pilot occurred. Lt. Ettinger had been released to the Bigboy team by an alleged North Korean general officer who claimed to be an operative of the partisan forces. This operations lasted from September 1951 until it was officially considered compromised and dropped after the helicopter sent in to rescue Ettinger was ambushed by enemy forces around the landing area. The BIGBOY operation was closed out in February 1952.[29]

This operation had in addition to its collection and reporting mission, to also scout out drop zones and provide reception committees for newly dropped personnel. During the month of February as the plan unfolded to rescue Lt. Ettinger, I recall making at least two resupply drops to BIGBOY. The second resupply drop contained material and instructions for the rescue. I particularly remember the BIGBOY drop zone because the approach to it required flying over the coastline directly toward the mountains. The planning was closely coordinated with the pilot and navigator because time over the drop zone was severely limited to permit the aircraft to break suddenly either right or left and to begin climbing over the prevailing mountain peaks. The prevailing winds greatly effected the approach and climbout. As I recall, the pilots were not happy to fly these missions.[30]

Before BIGBOY was dropped, it also participated in another mission to provide a reception committee near Wonsan for a two-man agent team with BIGBOY marking the drop zone with signal fires. Needless to say, this team never reported in after the drop.

Finally, the GREEN DRAGON operation as the largest scale operation so far, would drop 97 partisans from 3 C-119 aircraft west of Pyongyang on January 15, 1953 and were reinforced on 18/19 May 1953 with 56 partisans and large supplies of arms and equipment. This operation with many earmarks of compromise continued to operate culminating in an aborted mission to conduct a Snatch pickup of downed airforce personnel. The aircraft was almost shot down by small arms fire.[31]

I have not been able to locate any data that would indicate any type of operations audit or details of any investigative effort to determine compromise of these operations nor any of the other airborne missions where the dropped personnel simply disappeared.

The nature of these compromises is considered comparative with Special Operations Executive activities of World War II. The specific case involves the Dutch Resistance operatives and their wholesale compromise that led to the almost total destruction of the British airborne division and the Polish airborne brigade. The German success in compromising the Dutch resistance operation hinged on three facets of counter-espionage: decipher, interception and double agents. A Dutch intelligence agent, operating for the Dutch and M16, called Zomer, was arrested in the late summer of 1941 with a large pile of back messages from which the German's cipher expert was able to work out M16's cipher system. On February 13, 1942 two more M16 agents, Ter Laak and Van der Reyden, were arrested; Van der Ryden was so angry and so upset at getting caught that he said a great deal more than he might have when he was interrogated. The interrogator was also the recipient of the captured cipher data so he was more effective in the interrogation.[32]

With the help of a double agent, the Germans closed in on an SOE group. The Germans would never have had the successes they did in Holland without the aid of these Dutch informers who pretended to be resisters, but in fact, worked for the occupiers (Germans).[33]

The foregoing comparisons certainly beg the question of security compromises in many of the clandestine airborne executed in Korea during the war. When one takes into consideration the magnitude of mission failures, coupled with the foregoing description of the effectiveness of the Soviet integrated air defense system that tricked US Airforce responses to bogus electronic transmissions, why were none of the troop carrier, slow flying aircraft that flew countless missions all over North Korea not attacked by the MIGs? Taking into consideration the total control the Germans were able to effect over the Dutch Resistance movement in Holland, it would appear the Communists had developed an overall agent/partisan interception plan. Execution of such a plan could have determined it was more efficient and effective to find the drop zone locations by radar tracking and perhaps double agents rather than destroying the aircraft and its human cargo. Perhaps the plan should have been to do as the Germans did and let the drops occur, capture the personnel, decipher their codes and double the operation. In so doing, the Communist forces also determined UN intelligence requirements (Essential Elements of Information -EEIs), neutralized the insurgent threats, and benefited from the supplies, both medical and food stuffs as well as funds carried by the agents[34]

The foregoing conceptual analysis for the large scale of compromises of clandestine airborne operations is offered for the reader to consider. I was a part of this operation and flew 110 behind the line missions, at night, flying at low altitudes in the mountainous areas over North Korea. After taking such risks then I hope it was not in vain.

When I started writing this book I had concerns about documenting the suspicions I held regarding the compromise of the clandestine airborne special operations. I have already outlined my very strong feelings about such compromises and just recently I became aware of a Russian publication that tends to support my suspicions. This document provides evidence of direct Soviet participation in a successful counter-guerrilla program, directed against the United Nations forces of which my unit, the 8240th Army Unit was a principal element.

The translated Russian document I refer to is titled: "Russia (USSR) In Local Wars and Regional Conflicts In the Second Half of the 20th Century". Major General V. A. Zolotarev, editor in chief, V.A. Yaremenko, A. N. Pochtarev, authors, "Kuchkovo Polye" Publishing, Moscow 2000, 576 pages, ISBN 5-86090-065-1.South Korean

In Part I: Local Wars and Armed Conflicts in which Soviet and Russian Forces Have Participated, Chapter 2: Military-Political and Military-Strategic Support to Local Wars and Armed Conflicts, under- In the Far East and Southeast Asia (pp, 62-7), the evidence of Soviet military direction of the counter-guerrilla effort is established. Although in this reference only one counter-guerrilla operation is mentioned, it leads one to assume that the Soviet Military Advisors were very effective in neutralizing many other operations. This is proven by the great losses of agents and partisans, especially among those who were dispatched via clandestine airborne special operations.

From the referenced document, it appears that the Soviet Union made a conscious decision to support the North Korean invasion of South Korea, but feared Soviet Forces participating in the Korean War could cause a crisis in the military-political situation in Europe. For example such military action in Korea could be treated the same as an offensive by the Soviets in Europe. Drawing on that the leadership of the Soviet Union made a decision that only a limited number of Soviet military advisors would enter North Korea to accompany the Korean Peoples' Army (KPA) and the South Korean Partisans. By the start of the Korean War Soviet advisors were located with the Ministry of Defense, North Korea, as well as with the North Korean Military commands at most Levels. Certainly Soviet Military Intelligence advisors were also present.

It was due in large part to the efforts of the Soviet military advisors that the Korean Peoples' Army was created. Aided by the Soviet General staff, they developed all of the KPA operational plans in case of war on the Korean peninsula and also conducted reconnaissance in the areas of the 38th parallel. One must remember that even after the withdrawal of Soviet forces at the end of World War II, the Soviets made a decision to keep 4,293 military specialists in North Korea. Knowing that internal security and control of the populace is of paramount importance to a Communist form of government

One can assume that among these Soviet military advisors were many well-placed intelligence and counter-intelligence specialists. After the start of the Korean War on June 25, 1095, these Soviet Military advisors, all of who were located with the front line commanders and the Commanding General of the KPA, Kim Il Sung, Kim Il Sung, as well as with the rear guard units and formations. These Soviet Military advisors were strictly forbidden from crossing the 38th parallel for the duration of the war.

The referenced document reveals two scientific and technical intelligence requirements the Soviets had assigned the highest priority. One was the capture of the F-86, Sabre Jet. In a recent article by Ralph Wetterhand in the Retired Officer magazine, November edition 2003, titled: "The Unreturned", Wetterhand points out that even today the majority of missing prisoners of war-downed pilots are Sabre jet pilots. It is alleged that at least one F-86 pilot was taken to Moscow and debriefed. The Soviets were so eager to capture an F-86 that they established a special group: "NORD," consisting of twelve top Soviet pilots who were assigned the mission of capturing an F86. After several attempts in dogfights with USAF pilots in which one of the Soviet test pilots was killed, the project was abandoned and the pilots reassigned. Eventually, a forced landing of a damaged F-86 on a beach of the Yellow Sea provided the Soviets their prize a Sabre jet.

The second reference to successful Soviet planned and directed counter-guerrilla operations that netted the helicopter is highlighted in the document, but does not provide any details. The document reveals that two Soviet Military advisors were decorated for such an operation.

On 7 February 1952, the two Soviet military advisors planned and carried out the successful capture of an American helicopter. Lt. Colonels A. Glukov and L. Smirnov were recognized at the highest level in the Soviet government. By order of the Supreme Soviet of the USSR Lt. Colonel Glukov was awarded the Order of Lenin and Lt. Colonel Smirnov received the Order of the Red Banner. Assisting in the removal of the helicopter was a Colonel A. Dmitriev, Advisor and Senior Translator Lieutenant Nekhrapov. The helicopter was taken to Antung, inside the Chinese territory.

In both instances, the intelligence collection requirement was completed; the first due to aerial combat and a damaged aircraft, while the second requirement required the use of ground elements of a clandestine nature and a ruse the Americans would buy into. The Soviets probably assumed US forces always gave the highest priority to rescue downed airman, even at the risk of losing more personnel in the process.

The lure of the helicopter was in response to a radio message from the agents in the area that composed the BIG BOY operation. Although there had been some suspicions of its compromise, when the opportunity presented itself to rescue a downed pilot, security considerations fell by the wayside. I have addressed this operation earlier in the book about Navy Lt. Ettinger, who had been shot down and captured. He had been taken over by an alleged friendly North Korean General who was supposedly on the partisans' payroll. The general in turn turned over control to the BIG BOY agents to assist in and coordinate the helicopter rescue. The helicopter effected by ground fire from the trap that had been laid out and the damaged the blades caused the helicopter to crash, but was salvaged by the Soviets. So, once again, the Soviets satisfied two collection requirements. The first with the F-86 due to its damaged, the second, the helicopter by means of a compromised clandestine operation successfully used against UN/US forces.

Undoubtedly, sometime in the future more documents will be discovered or made available that will detail some of the Soviet counter-guerrilla operations. Certainly one can assume from the foregoing that the Soviets counter-offensive intelligence operations in Korea was principally responsible for the large scale losses of agents and partisans that were dispatched into North Korea by the US Intelligence units. The GREEN DRAGON operation covered earlier in the book was no doubt compromised by the Soviets counter-guerrilla plan, as well as, the operation to once again respond to a rescue of downed airmen from a B-29. In that case the aircraft that was to utilize the Snatch Pickup method became another potential loss, but the pilot was engaged perhaps too early by ground fire and was able to successfully abort the operation.

Earlier in my analysis I alluded to the effectiveness of the Soviet Integrated Air Defense Capability to monitor any aircraft, once airborne, from areas of South Korea and then track the aircraft thereby alerting North Korean and Chinese forces of it track and perhaps destination This also provided Soviet Military advisors directing the counter-guerrilla program to quickly respond with ground security forces and seize our personnel assuming the Soviets had not already penetrated the operation before it got off the ground. With that twin capability there is no wonder so many clandestine special operations were lost.

CHAPTER XI

EPILOGUE

In the beginning of my research I started to expand upon the conditions leading up to the Korean War, and the political aspects of the Truman Administration when it failed to include Korea as part of the United States sphere of interest in Asia. However, after reading and reviewing references contained in the bibliography, I decided to limit the scope of this book to only the clandestine airborne operational efforts, its inherent failures as well as its successes. I am sure some details are not covered and for that I apologize. I am aware that some readers may be more knowledgeable of these activities than I.

I found my assignment to AVIARY as well as to the TLO team with the First Marine Division to be intriguing, and the type assignment that comes to a soldier perhaps once in his career. Additionally, the assignment was a professional challenge that required not only aggressively pursuing the war, but also to exert every skill and technique imaginable to ensure the safety of the lives of the personnel involved.

To this very day, I have had concern for the Korean patriots that displayed unimaginable courage and fortitude to engage in this kind of warfare. As the 50th Anniversary of the Korean War activities developed, I immediately organized the 8240th Army Unit Commemorative Committee with the purpose of locating and starting a dialogue between the US veterans and the surviving Korean agents and partisans. To that end, I visited Korea in September 2000, accompanied by my wife and daughter. The Korean partisans, 350 strong, warmly greeted my family and me and made us feel at home with them.

The Korean War Veterans Federation of 8240th Army Unit, United Nations Partisan Forces had designed their own medal to recognize their veterans. The medal is the Korean Partisan Honor Medal. I was presented 300 of the medals to present to the US Veterans, as they are located. These US veterans are now exchanging letters with many of the Korean partisans still living in Korea. This is but one of many more initiatives I have planned to support the drawing together of the two veterans groups just as it was during the war.

Now to address some of the points recorded in the book pertaining to the clandestine airborne effort. One must understand the environment that existed in June 1950 when the Korean War began. Specifically, the capabilities of the existing airborne experienced personnel both with the US Army and the US Airforce and National Defense budget reductions. A familiar phrase that my University of Maryland professors continually alluded to in their discussions of United States Foreign Policy was the nation's proclivity to drastically reduce defense budgets in peacetime. Thus, the creditability of the United States military strength to support its foreign policy, especially by the Soviet Union, certainly influenced the Korean War.

The 82d Airborne Division then was the so called "strategic force" in the United States, and commented upon earlier in this book, until the outbreak of the Korean War, the 82d normally had only the US Airforce Liaison Officer's C47 to use for paratroopers pay jumps. Therefore, in the Far East absolutely no airborne element existed to conduct any type airborne missions.

As the North Korean People's Army successfully pushed the meager US forces back into the Pusan perimeter, wheels began turning of how to react with appropriate forces. The l87th Regimental Combat Team, Airborne, was assembled at Fort Campbell and hastily dispatched to South Korea. Additionally the Ranger Infantry Companies (Airborne) were organized, trained equally in a hasty manner and dispatched to South Korea. Upon their arrival in Korea, then a cadre of airborne, combat experienced personnel provided a source of personnel to staff the clandestine airborne effort. However, these units were not for that purpose. Although, the Far East Command directed the establishment of the AVIARY team in August 1950, it did not have personnel experienced in such operations. So the conceptualization and execution began under the control of 1st Lieutenant Robert Brewer. Without experienced staff personnel to analyze and even question the viability of the AVIARY missions, many were failures with an unconscionable loss of indigenous personnel and logistical support coming only after the front-line units were served.

With this picture in mind, one must realize that the units and personnel needed to react to this war did not exist, another facet of the budgets was further reduced. This was a syndrome that existed in the period from 1946 to 1950. Therefore, the military services simply husbanded resources to support forces in Europe during that time period. First because the "Iron Curtain" of Europe occupied the time and resources of the politicos and senior military leaders perceived the threat to peace was in Europe not Asia. Also the perception of a need for any type of special operations units probably, if on any planners list, was at the bottom of it.

While these conditions existed at the beginning of the Korean War there was an immediate necessity to immediately reinforce the US Eighth Army at the same time it was fighting for its very life. Hence, the priority of support was developed for these newly dispatched front-line divisions to hold the Pusan perimeter until more help arrived. Even with that situation, the AVIARY started up and began dropping intelligence agents. Again, an effort was created in combat with meager resources and limited experienced leadership. Its failures are easy to criticize, but one must walk in Lt. Brewer's shoes, to begin to understand the pressures on all operational elements fighting in Korea. At the same time the US Airforce was experiencing similar problems. As addressed in Mike Haas' book, IN THE DEVIL'S SHADOW, the troop carrier pilots were flying routine transport and personnel flights during the day, and nighttime classified missions after their day was done. This led to the set-up of the B-Flight for Special Missions. This airforce realignment of air support came only after the weaknesses of the earlier failures were analyzed so effective corrective action could be taken by the army and airforce entities that were involved in the clandestine airborne effort.

While the AVIARY team pursued intelligence activities, the availability of partisans for behind the lines operations facilitated the development of the BAKER SECTION and its operations. However, as seen in the coverage of selected clandestine airborne operations such as VIRGINIA I and SPITFIRE, the BAKER SECTION operations seemed to be ad hoc developments as seen with personnel, such as the British officers walking in off the street, and establishing their own bona fides. Evidently, the pressures of combat overcame the systematic development of an organized effort staffed with experienced personnel. For example, the BAKER SECTION had to borrow Rangers to conduct their first mission. We see in the case of the B-26 shootdown, and the loss of Lewis and Hearn as well as the pilot, that mission combined two missions, one of which only Lewis knew the real purpose and was stimulated by an outside agency. The preparation for that mission was certainly ad hoc. According to my discussions with Major David Sharp, British Army, a POW in the same camp Lewis was targeting, told me an Infantry Regimental size force moved into the area of the camp just before the B-26 shootdown. It would seem that to check on the creditability of the initial source of information that General Dean was in the camp, which a parallel intelligence collection operation would have been done. No doubt it would have detected the presence of the regiment, thereby, indicating a possible ambush of the aerial reconnaissance.

Now to address the pool or cadre of airborne qualified, combat experienced personnel alluded to above. It would seem that someone in the US Eighth Army staff, possibly the G-1, G-2 and the G-3 working together with Colonel McGee, could have worked out an arrangement with command support for either the 187th or Ranger Companies. This arrangement could have provided cadre to Colonel McGee's Miscellaneous Group, and to BAKER SECTION which was his subordinate operational arm. Recall Colonel McGee did borrow Captain Channon, a Ranger, to clear up a problem with the offshore partisans and the four Rangers to conduct operation VIRGINIA I.

One can only speculate that the Ranger Companies being assigned to the front-line divisions where each company had distinguished itself in combat, that the Division Commander would resist efforts to take away any of the strengths of his Ranger Company. This would be especially true if the Ranger Company Commander opposed the loss of any of his Rangers or if the Division staff discovered it and advised the Commander. Another alternative would have been the assignment of a Ranger Company to BAKER SECTION as it arrived in country that would have provided the type airborne and small unit's combat knowledge a partisan unit needed. Cadre from the 187th was probably not considered after its commander BG Trapnell personally rejected the transfer Captain Channon as requested by MG Jack Singlaub (then Major of the CIA element).

As the war continued and the detailed assessment was completed, the clandestine airborne operation evolved into one entity, AVIARY. Personnel selection program was setup and the logistical system established. Even through the operational executions improved in the aerial delivery of personnel and equipment, the failure rate did not end.

Subsequent to the Korean War duty, I became a member of the US Army Intelligence Corps. In such capacity and experience in an assignment at the US Army Intelligence School, Fort Holabird, Maryland, there I learned in greater detail the evolution of the Communist society and its internal security measures. With that knowledge and having reviewed the conduct of the Korean operations, I am surprised that any of the clandestine airborne operations succeeded, especially after the front-line stabilized. The Communists expanded their internal security forces to identify, collate the data, and essentially control the daily lives of every person in North Korea. Also, the incentive to report on one's neighbor or the punishment for aiding any anticommunist person or activity most likely accounts for the high rate of agent/partisan losses. The other losses can also be attributed to compromises caused by North Korean agents or double agents. I do not believe our forces understood the nature of Communist internal controls and their influence on locals turning in our agents and partisans.

Finally, the courage and demonstrated patriotism of these agents and partisans also indicated that they believed in the effort, unless they were double agents simply returning to North Korea and there were some. These patriots placed their trust in the US personnel who trained and jumped them into North Korea. This part is difficult to accept without heartfelt feelings for their death, torture and or imprisonment due to our activities. The US veterans who worked with these patriots should join in a concerted effort to influence US official recognition and some form of compensation.

In the year 2001 we have seen another clandestine airborne operation performed by the US Army Rangers on a raid against a Taliban stronghold. It was a classic night jump, quick striking the target and then exfiltrating via helicopters. Who would have assumed in these current times that the same type and mode of transportation would be employed once again, as BAKER SECTION AND AVIARY did over fifty years ago!

However, not to be over shadowed are the initially reported actions of the small Special Forces Teams in action in Afghanistan. Captain Jason Amerine, commanding the initial SF team, described his team's entry into Afghanistan. An 11-man team from the 5th SF Group went in at night in October. They dropped into a valley deep inside Taliban territory in central Afghanistan. Out of the darkness stepped Hamid Karzi, who later was designated acting leader of the new Afghanistan government. The subsequent actions of this SF team in directing airstrikes and defending themselves with the local opposition forces is reminiscent of the actions taken by Ranger Sgt. Miles while on Operation SPITFIRE he observed and directed airstrikes on new Chinese Communist Division elements moving south toward the front-line. This was a clandestine airborne operation that again delivered the Special Operations team directly into battle even though it was done fifty year after Operation Spitfire. Captain Amerine and three other members of his team were interviewed on television at Ramstein AFB, Germany on December 10, 2001.

The command structure and planning is now very professional. The Joint Special Operations (SOCOM) commanded by a full General with each of the military services own special operations commands can effectively deploy their operational special operations forces. For example, the US Army has the US Army Rangers, Special Forces and Delta Force, the Navy has its Sea Air Land (SEALS) and the Airforce has its Air Commandos to augment whatever commitment may be assigned on a worldwide scope.

This super special operations command structure is a far cry from the days in Korea when initiative and field expedients had to be employed while engaging in an active major land war.

Appendix A

GLOSSARY

AIC	U. S. Army grouping of Intelligence and Counter Intelligence Personnel into an Intelligence Corp.
AERIAL RECON	Flights over a designated area of Interest
AVIARY	Airborne operational element that trained and dropped agents and partisans behind the lines in North Korea
BAKER SECTION	Eighth US Army Guerrilla and Special Airborne Operations Activity
BEMNT	Beginning of Early Morning Nautical Twilight
Blueboy	Code name for X Corps Intelligence Collection element
CIA	Central Intelligence Agency
CCRAK	Combined Command, Reconnaissance Activities-Korea
CCF	Chinese Communist Forces
CCVPA	Chinese Communist Volunteer People's Army
CW	Morse code used by radio operators vice voice
DISPLAY PANELS	Air-ground communications system
DoD	Department of Defense
DONKEY	Code name for partisan operational teams that were numbered, ie. Donkey 1, etc.
DZ	Drop zone or landing area for the jumpers.
EEI	Essential Elements of Information
E&E	Escape and Evasion
EUSAK	Eighth U.S. Army serving in Korea
EXFILTRATION	Escaping from enemy territory by foot, air or water using evasive tactics and stealth to avoid capture
FAC	Forward Air Controller directs combat air support
FEAF	Far East Airforces

FEC U.S.	Far East Command
FEC-G2	Far East Command Intelligence Directorate
FEC/LD (K)	Far East Command Liaison Detachment (Korea)
FEC/LG	Far East Command Liaison Group
FEBA	Forward Edge of the Battle Area
FLAK PAD	Rectangular shaped pads of nylon reinforced to protect against small arms and anti-aircraft shell fragments. Usually placed on the floor of the aircraft.
INFILTRATION	Ground by foot, Air by air drop, seaborne landings using stealth and secretive movement to gain access to enemy occupied areas.
G-1	US Army staff designation for Personnel/ Administration
G-2	US Army staff designation for Intelligence
G-3	US Army staff designation for Operations
JACK	Joint Advisory Commission-Korea (CIA)
JATO	Jet Assisted Take-off for Seaplanes
JUMPMASTER	Usually the senior paratrooper on the aircraft who controls the actual jumping of personnel aboard.
KIA	Killed in action
KLO	Korean Labor Organization
KMAG	Korean Military Advisory Group
MAE WEST	W.W.II Soldier's reference to a Life Preserver
MAP RECON	An extensive study of aerial photographs and maps of an area of interest
MISSING IN ACTION	Combat personnel unaccounted for after an action
MLR	Main Line of Resistance
MSR	Main supply route utilized by military forces
NKPA	North Korean People's Army
OB	Order of battle information on the enemy forces
OPLR	Outpost Line of Resistance
PARA-MARINE	Airborne qualified Marine
PARTISAN	Friendly irregular forces Vs Guerrilla

	enemy forces
PATHFINDER	Advance group of paratroopers who land on the DZ and guide in the remaining flights to drop troops or supplies
PAYJUMP	To receive jump pay each paratrooper must jump every three months.
PLA	People's Liberation Army (China)
PRC-10	Portable Radio Communications, set model 10
PW	Prisoner of War
REPLACEMENT CENTER	US Army facility processing replacements
ROK	Republic of Korea
ROKA	Republic of Korea Army
SA-17	Seaplane
SAM	Special Air Missions
SAS	British Special Air Service (Equivalent to US SF)
SCR-300	Signal Corps Radio, Set 300
SMG	Special Missions Group (CIA)
SOFT NOSED	The nose of a B-26 Bomber fitted with plexi glass. Bubble like cover from where the navigator can observe the terrain over, around and below the aircraft to aid in navigation.
SPITFIRE	The partisan code name for the operation conducted in North Korea in March 1951
TARGETS OF OPPORTUNITY	Targets not preplanned but become exposed
TLO	Tactical Liaison Office
UN	United Nations
UNPFK	United Nations Partisan Forces Korea
UW	Unconventional Warfare (Irregular Forces are used)
VIRGINIA	Code name for an airborne partisan operation in North Korea conducted in June 1951
WW II	World War Two

Appendix B - Partisan Unit Insignias and Badges

Appendix C - Rules of Encouragement of Capturing the Wanted American Imperialist Agents Through Reward

Summary of "Rules for Encouragement of Capturing the Wanted American Imperialist Agents through Reward" published by Peng Te-huei, Commander-in-Chief, the People's Volunteer Army of Communist China on May 15, 1952:

(1) One of two "agents" with Chinese nationality captured alive by the frontline troops: The company commander and platoon leader thereof shall be respectively distinguished with two grand merits, the squad leader and soldiers thereof shall be respectively distinguished with one grand merit, and all of them distinguished as such sahll be transferred to the rear area for 6-month rest and recuperation; if captured by the rear area troops, the said commander, leaders and soldiers thereof shall be respectively distinguished with grand merit and transferred to Manchuria for 3-month rest and recuperation.

(2) If they are captured alive by the "local officials" or the people, a reward of RMB8,000,000 (old RMB) shall be paid to these officials or people.

Remarks:

(1) According to the broadcasting by the People's Broadcasting Station of Communist China in Pyengyang (News Summary recorded at 0800 hours on May 15, 1952).

(2) Such a public notice was posted at various traffic control points in North Korea.

大專全公 華 國 翻 評 社
CATHAY. TRANSLATION SERVICE
UNDER THE 7TH FLOOR. FIRST CO., LTD.
144 MINGCHUAN STREET, SEC. 1, TAIPEI, TAIWAN

TEL: (02)382-1342
台北市漢口街一段一四四號
第一公司七樓七〇三室

Appendix D - Capture of American Imperialist Agent Wang Chi

A report on the captured Chinese warriors in Korean War (the agents
for UN Corps behind enemy area) by the Communist China (Appeared on
Page 1 of Southern Daily in Communist China dated March 28, 1953):

   (Headline)   American Imperialist Airborne Agent Wang Chi
                Captured by the People's Volunteer Army Troops

   The said agents, totalled 9, were sent by the American imperialist for collecting intelligence concerning the effect of bacterial
agent. As a result of searching for their bodies, some bugging devices, signal pigeons, military maps and carbines were discovered.

        (Content)   Criminal Evidence

   (Frontline, Korea, 26 March 1953, New China News Agency) At 0730
hours on March 15, 1953, our People's Volunteer Army troops captured
an airborne agent (code-named as Wang Chih-chia) who was sent by the
American imperialist for collecting the intelligence in relation to
the effect of bacterial agent on the hill nearby Shih Cheng Tung, Kou
Erh Area, Kimchon County. As one of the American imperialist airborne
agents captured by our troops recently, Wang Chi is now 21 years old,
a native of Chuchi Hsien, Chekiang Province, China, a member of Chiang
Kai-shek's "Patriotic Youth" (namely Anti-Communist and Resis-Russia
Corps), and an agent of "Headquarters Far East Command Liaison Detachment" of American imperialist who is aggressing against Korea, wears
Chinese Communist Forces uniform and pretended as a field artillery
surveyor of our troops. It is found that the characters U.S. were
printed in black on the inner liners at the armpits of sleeves of his
overcoat and cotton-padded jacket and that a cross was tattooed on
his left arm.

   According to his own confession, Wang Chi and other 8 agents
(all are Chinese) who were assigned by "8240th Army Unit, Headquarters
Far East Command Liaison Detachment (Korea)" took off by two 2-engine
transporters from Souel at 1830 hours on March 14 and dropped in our
area. His team consisted of 5 agents. These 9 agents were given the
mission of investigating the effect of bacterial agent at 0800 hours
on March 13. They are supposed to investigate these matters: Which
infectious diseases happened in North Korea? Are there many flies,
fleas and rats in the area where the infectious diseases happened?
How about the status of infectious extent, mortality and plague control therein? and to accomplish their mission in two weeks. The
articles they brought with themselves include the forged official seal,
passes and immunity certificates of our People's Volunteer Army troops,
bugging devices, signal pigeons, military maps and carbines.

武原立業　華　國　翻　譯　社
公益標義

CATHAY TRANSLATION SERVICE

TEL:(02)382-1342

台北市漢口街一段一四四號
第一公司七樓七○三室

NOTES

General comments regarding this book. Although much of the information in this book is a bibliographical collection of my experience as well as a compilation of information from other sources, many of the other sources' experiences were also shared by me. For the other sources due credit must be recorded for their contributions.

Introduction

1. The description of this critical resupply mission to the DONKEY 15 partisans was compiled from the mutual experiences of Major Emory Albritton , US Army and me. Both of us participated in this mission.
2. Discussions with Albritton and video taping May 2001.
3. Author's firsthand knowledge as jumpmaster on this mission.

CHAPTER I
Evolution of Clandestine Airborne Operations (Korea)

1. Cleaver, et al., <u>UN Partisan Warfare in Korea, 1951-1953</u>, 52-53
2. Evanhoe, <u>Dark Moon. Eighth Army Special Operations in the Korean War</u>.
3. Malcom, <u>WhiteTigers, My Secret War in North Korea</u>.
4. Author's personal experience.
5. Armellino, phone interview and letter to author dtd May 1, 2001.
6. Evanhoe, <u>Dark Moon</u>, 50-62.
7. IBID.
8. IBID.
9. IBID.
10. Brewer and Author's experience in airborne operations.
11. Trest, <u>Air Commando One</u>, 32-33.
12. IBID, 31.

CHAPTER II
Strategy and Techniques

1. Author's and Major Albritton's personal experiences.
2. IBID.
3. Armellino, Interview and letter to author, May 1, 2001.
4. Author and Captain Armellino's discussions. May 2001.
5. IBID.
6. IBID.
7. IBID.

8. IBID.

9. IBID.

10. Carver, Robert, Jr. debriefing of mission by author, Seoul, 1952.

11. Palmer, Ralph, discussions and documentation provided to author.

12. Haas, <u>In the Devil's Shadow: U.S. Special Operations During the Korean War</u>, 94.

13. Armellino, interview by author, May 2001.

CHAPTER III
Personnel Staffing

1. Author's personal experience.

2. Evanhoe, <u>Dark Moon</u>, 47-48.

3. IBID.

4. IBID.

5. Armellino interview and letter to author, May 1, 2001.

6. Albritton, discussions with author, May 2001.

7. Author's personal experience.

8. Channon, discussions with author, Sept. 2001, Bowie, Md.

9. Author's experience and discussions with 8240 veterans at October 2000 reunion.

10. Watts, <u>Korean Knights, 4th Ranger Infantry Company (Abn)</u>, 296.

11. Evanhoe, <u>Dark Moon</u>, 61.

CHAPTER IV
Logistics

1. Author's personal experience.

2. Albritton, Letter 1951 (LS-51) and Cleaver, et al. (Logistics GHQ Letter for 8240th AU).

3. IBID.

4. Author's experience.

CHAPTER V
Courageous Courier

1. Pratt, <u>Courageous Courier</u>, 128 (Author discussions with 1st Corps Pigeon Handlers).

2. Author's experience.

3. IBID.

4. Pratt, 68.

5. IBID.

6. IBID.

7. The Washington Post, November 27, 2000.

CHAPTER VI
Selected Clandestine Airborne Operations

VIRGINIA I

1. Evanhoe, <u>Dark Moon</u>, 50-51.
2. Watts, <u>Korean Knights</u>, 109.
3. Evanhoe, <u>Dark Moon</u>, 52-53.
4. IBID.
5. IBID.
6. IBID.
7. Watson, Debriefing Report, ID-950774.
8. IBID.
9. IBID.
10. Evanhoe, <u>Dark Moon</u>, 58.
11. IBID.
12. IBID, (Also related to passages in John Thornton's book).
13. IBID.
14. Watson, Debriefing Report, ID-950774

SPITFIRE

1. Anderson, <u>Banner Over Pusan</u>, 62-78.
2. Evanhoe, <u>Dark Moon</u>, 109.
3. IBID.
4. Author's observations from an intelligence viewpoint.
5. Evanhoe, <u>Dark Moon</u>, 107.
6. IBID.
7. IBID.
8. IBID.
9. IBID.
10. IBID.
11 Author's observations.
12. Evanhoe, <u>Dark Moon</u>, 109 and Anderson, <u>Banner over Pusan</u>, 82-85.
13. Anderson, <u>Banner over Pusan</u>, 139-156.
14. Evanhoe, <u>Dark Moon</u>.
15. IBID.
16. IBID.
17. IBID.
18. Author's observation.
19. Evanhoe, <u>Dark Moon</u>.
20. IBID.

AVIARY'S FIRST GREAT LOSS AND SHOOTDOWN OF THE B-26.

1. Author's personal experience.
2. Evanhoe, <u>Dark Moon</u>, 142-144.
3. IBID.
4. Author's personal experience.
5. Evanhoe, <u>Dark Moon</u>, 121-123.
6. Lewis, Author interview Sept. 2002 and Video taping.and telephone calls to Pelzer.
7. Author's knowledge.
8. Author's discussions with Lewis, Sept. 2000.
9. IBID.

USE OF THE B-26 BOMBER AND THE COMMUNIST AIR DEFENSE.

1. Author's knowledge and experience in Korea.
2. IBID (Also comments by Futtel, <u>The US Airforce in Korea</u>).
3. Wetterhahn, <u>The Russians of MIG Alley</u>, TROA Article, Aug. 2000.
4. Author's experience and discussions with Captain Armellino.
5. IBID.

GREEN DRAGON.

1. Evanhoe, <u>Dark Moon</u>, 158-159.
2. Spangler, et al, <u>Guerrilla Warfare and Airpowers in Korea</u>, 146-149.
3. Author discussions with 82440th Veterans Oct 2000, Reunion Panama City Beach, FL.
4. Haas, 104.

CHAPTER VII
Overall Review of Clandestine Airborne Operations

1. Author's observations.
2. Haas, 23-24.
3. Cleaver, et al., 52.
4. IBID.
5. Author's observations.
6. IBID.
7. Evanhoe, 158.
8. IBID.
9. Author's observations.
10. Evanhoe, 158-159.
11. IBID.
12. IBID.
13. IBID.

CHAPTER VIII
Personal Histories- AVIARY Personnel and Others

1. Armellino, interview and letter to author.
2. Swanson, letter to author.
3. Blair, Life Magazine article, July 28, 1952.
4. Albritton, personal letter to author.
5. Chada, interview and personal papers to author.
6. Palmer, discussions and personal papers sent to author.
7. Dillard, personal experience and documentation.

CHAPTER IX
Recapitulation of U. S. Airforce Special Operations, Korea

1. Marion, US Airforce Special Operations Korean War Chronology, 1-20.
2. Dillard, author's comments.
3. Trest, Air Commando One, 30-31.
4. Dillard, author's comments.

CHAPTER X
Analysis of Clandestine Airborne Operations

1. Evanhoe, Dark Moon, 47-48.
2. Watts, Korean Knights, 359-360.
3. Dillard, author's comments.
4. Watts, Korean Knights, 296-298.
5. IBID.
6. Dillard, author's comments.
7. Anderson, Banner Over Pusan.
8. Dillard, author's comments.
9. IBID.
10. IBID.
11. Cleaver, UN Partisan Warfare in Korea, 1951-1954, 52-53.
12. Marion, US Airforce Special Operations Korean Chronology.
13. Dillard, author's Comments.
14. Trest, Air Commando One, 26-27
15. Dillard, author's comments.
16. Armellino, letter to author, May 2001.
17. Dillard, author's comments.
18. Evanhoe, Dark Moon, 55-56.
19. Cleaver, et al., 17.
20. Dillard, author's comments.

21. IBID.
22. Wetterhahn, <u>The Russians in MIG Alley</u>, (TROA Magazine Article.
23. McGill, <u>Black Tuesday over NAMSI</u>, (VFW Magazine Article).
24. Wetterhahn, <u>The Russians in MIG Alley</u>.
25. IBID.
26. IBID.
27. Dillard, author's comments.
28. US Eighth Army Reports, October 1951.
29. Evanhoe, <u>Dark Moon</u>, 141.
30. Dillard, author's comments.
31. Marion, <u>US Airforce Special Operations Korean Chronology</u>.
32. Foot, <u>The Special Operations Executive, 1940-46</u>, 130-132.
33. IBID.
34. Dillard, author's comments.

Selected Bibliography

Primary Sources.

Albritton, Emory, Major, (r) US Army, Interviews and letter to author, Fayetteville, NC. 2000-2001.

Armellino, Richard A., Captain, USAF, Interview and Letter to author, Jacksonville, FL. May 1, 2001.

Carver, Robert, Jr., Corporal, US Army. Author debriefing, Seoul, Korea, 1952.

Chada, Orlando W, Sergeant, US Army, Telecon and Documentation provided to author, Eugene, OR, 2001.

Channon, Robert I, Colonel, (r) US Army. Interview Bowie, Maryland, and Sept 27, 2001.

Evenhoe, Ed. Dark Moon: Eight Army Special Operations in the Korean War, Naval Institute Press, Annapolis 1995.

Foot, M.R.D. SOE: The Special Operations Executive 1940-46. British Broadcasting Corporation, London. 1984.

Futrell, Robert F. The United States Air Force in Korea, 1950-1953, Rec. ed. Office of Airforce History, Washington, 1983.

Haas, Michael E. Colonel, (r) USAF, In The Devil's Shadow, United States Special Operations During The Korean War. Naval Institute Press, Annapolis, 2000.

Hong, John. (Partisan). Interview by author in Washington DC. July 2001.

Lewis, William. LTC, (r), US Army. Interview and Video taping, Bethesda, MD. September 2000.

Lim, Thomas H. (Partisan). Interview by author, Washington DC, July 2001.

Marion, Forrest L. Major, USAF, US Airforce Special Operations Korean Chronology.

McGill, Earl J. B-29 pilot in the Korean War. Author of article Black Tuesday Over Namsi. VFW Magazine, October 2001 edition.

Palmer, Ralph, SFC, US Army. Interview by author and documentation provided to author July 2001.

Pelser, Frederick P. LTC, (r) USAF. Freedom Bridge. Fairfield, CA, Fremar Press, 184. and telephone discussions between author and Pelser 2000.

Pratt, Jerome. LTC, (r), US Army. Courageous Couriers, Memoirs of a Pigeon Soldier. Frank H. Hollmann, Warrenton, MO. May 1977.

Sharp, David Major SAS, British Army, (r). Interviews by author September-October Panama City Beach, FL.

Spangler, Frank M, et. al. Guerrilla Warfare and Airpower in Korea, 1950-1954. Aerospace Studies Institute, Maxwell Airforce Base, AL. 1964.

Stanton, Shelby L. America's Tenth Legion, X Corps In Korea, 1950. Presido Press Novato, CA, 1989.

Swanson, Graham, Staff Lt. Royal Vany, (r). Letter to author from Swanson, United Kingdom, May 6, 2001.

Thornton, John W. Captain, (r) US Navy. Believed To Be Alive. Paul S. Erickson, Middlebury, VT. 1981.

Toland, John. In Mortal Combat. Morrow, New York. 1991.

Trest, Warren A. Air Commando One, Heine Aderholt and America's Secret Air Wars. Smithsonian Institution Press, Washington and London, 2000.

United States Army Files, CCRAK, Records Group 342. National Archives Washington, DC.

Watts, Joe C, Jr. Korean Knights, The 4th Ranger Infantry Company (ABN). 1950-1951. Southern Heritage Press, St. Petersburg, FL, 1997.

Wingate, Kingston, Colonel, (r) US Army. Interview by author, Fort Bragg, NC. July 2000.

Secondary Sources.

Anderson, Ellery, Captain, British Army, M.B.E., M.C. Banner Over Pusan, Adventure in Korea. Evans Brothers, London, 1960.

Blair, Clay. Robinson Crusoe of Schintz-Do. Life Magazine, July 28, 1952. New York.

Breuer, William B. Shadow Warriors, The Covert War In Korea. John Wiley and Sons, Inc. New York, 1996.

Cleaver, Frederick, and others. UN Partisan Warfare in Korea, 1951-1954. AFFE Group, Technical Memorandum ORO-T-64 AFFE, Operations Research Office, Johns Hopkins University, 1956.

Colgrove, Kenneth, Dr. Democracy versus Communism Series, No. 10, Communist and Colonization. D.Van Norstrand Company, Inc. Princeton, 1957, rev. 1961.

Goulden, Joseph C. Korea: The Untold Story of the War. New York Times Books, 1982.

Halliday, Jan. Air Operations in Korea: The Soviet Side of the Story. Imprint Publications, Chicago, 1993.

Hallion, Richard P. Naval Air Operations in Korea. Imprint Publications, Chicago, 1993.

Intelligence Information by Partisans for Armor. Vols. 1 and 2, Student Committee Report.

United States Armored Officer Advanced Course, Fort Knox, KY, 1952. Participants: LTC. Garth Stevens, Maj. Frank D. Bush, Capt. Robert Brewer. Capt. Jefferson DeR. Capps and Capt. Charles J. Simmons.

Malcom, Ben S. Colonel, (r) US Army. White Tigers, My Secret War in North Korea. Brassey's, Washington, D.C. 1996.

McGee, John H. Rice and Salt. Naylor, San Antonio, 1962.

Memorandum for Major General Willoughby, Korean Liaison Office Report. GHQ, Far East Command, APO 500, May 15, 1951.

Paschall, Rod. Colonel, (r) US Army. A Study in Command and Control: Special Operations In Korea, 1951-1953. Military History Institute, Carlisle Barracks, June 1988.

Schuetta, Lawrence V. Guerrilla Warfare and Airpower In Korea, 1950. Photocopy of Transcript, Aerospace Studies Institute, Maxwell AFB, AL. Jan. 1964.

U. S. Army Forces, Far East. <u>UN Partisan Forces In The Korean Conflict</u>. Military History Institute, Carlisle Barracks. MHD-3 Report, APO 301, 1954.

U. S. Army Field Manual No. 34-71. <u>Opposing Force Training Module: North Korean Military Forces</u>, Washington, DC. Feb. 5, 1982.

U. S. Army 2d Infantry Division. <u>Notes On The North Korean Army</u>. G-2/ Operations and Training, G2/Operations and Training, Korea, Nov. 4, 1982.

U. S. Army. <u>Military Characteristics of Airborne Equipment</u>. U. S. Army Quartermaster School, Fort Lee, Va. May 1954.

Wetterhahn, Ralph. <u>The Russians of MIG Alley</u>. The Retired Officers Magazine, Alexandria, Edition August 2000.

Printed in the United States
By Bookmasters